# WHO WILL GO FOR US?

An Invitation to Ordained
Ministry

# WHO WILL GO FOR US?

## DENNIS M. CAMPBELL

ABINGDON PRESS
NASHVILLE

WHO WILL GO FOR US?

*Copyright © 1994 Abingdon Press*

All rights reserved.

*This book is printed on acid-free recycled paper.*

**Library of Congress Cataloging-in-Publication Data**

Campbell, Dennis M., 1945–
  Who will go for us? : an invitation to ordained ministry / Dennis M. Campbell.
    p.  cm.
  Includes bibliographical references.
  ISBN 0-687-46775-6
  1. Clergy—Appointment, call, and election.  I. Title.
BV4011.4.C365  1994
253'.2—dc20                                                            93-23623
                                                                          CIP

00 01 02 03 —10 9 8 7

MANUFACTURED IN THE UNITED STATES OF AMERICA

# Contents

# You Are Invited

*The gifts he gave were that some would be apostles, some prophets, some evangelists, some pastors and teachers, to equip the saints for the work of ministry, for building up the body of Christ.*

—Ephesians 4:11-12

---

*"I will go, Lord, if you lead me. I will hold your people in my heart."*

—Dan Schutte, "Here I Am, Lord," 1981

After graduating from college, he joined the accounting firm of Price Waterhouse. A series of promotions made his future as an accountant seem assured. Now, however, he is in seminary preparing for the church's ordained ministry. "A very large part of my life has been spent trying to discern what God wants me to do. Should I devote my life to the church through my work as a CPA and through volunteer work in the community, or should I enter the ordained ministry and use my talents in pastoral ministry? No matter what, that question always came back, and I realized that all my questions about ordained ministry had to be answered." Reflecting further on the nature of his call, and the discussions he had with friends from the accounting firm, he observes, "Some people look at the life of ministry as what you're giving up, but I look at it as what I'm being given."

These comments are adapted from an interview with a theological student in *The Chronicle of Higher Education* (May 19, 1993). They are consistent with reports from many men and women who have sought to discern God's will for their lives in regard to ordained ministry. A consistent theme is the persistence of the question: "Is this what God and the church want me to do with my life?" Many wish the opportunity to consider the question had come earlier, perhaps while they were yet in school.

You are invited to think about the nature, role, and work of the ministry of the church. In our baptism, we all are called to lives of service in the world for God and other human beings. We share in the ministry of the church of Jesus Christ in various ways, through multiple roles.

From the earliest days of the church, some Christians have been called to a kind of leadership within the church which is called ordained ministry. Perhaps you are a student, in high school, college, or university, who is thinking about what you will do with your life, or a lay person, active in a Christian congregation, whose service there is causing you to wonder if you are called to ordained ministry. Perhaps you have been recognized and identified by a pastor, teacher, college chaplain, or friend as a person who should be challenged to think about the reality and possibility of the call of God and the church to ordained ministry. You may be a Christian who once considered ordained ministry and rejected it, but never has been satisfied by that rejection, and is willing to ponder again the nature of your vocation. You may be a person who is exploring a variety of ways to serve the church, in social service, foreign mission, education, music, or administration, and you are seeking to discern God's will as to whether you are called to the particular ministry of ordination.

Let it be said from the outset that I am not impartial. At a party I once encountered a friend. She asked what I was doing; and I told her I was working on a book about ordained ministry. She smiled and said, "I bet you come out in favor of it." I do. I believe that ordained ministry is a gift to the church from God; and that it is a great calling. It is a marvelous way to live one's life. The work of the ordained minister is enormously satisfying. I do not know of other vocations that are at once so significant, rewarding, and enjoyable.

A good case has not been made for the ordained ministry in our time. At some earlier periods in history churches gave great attention to recruiting for this ministry. Pastors, bishops, college chaplains, other church leaders, including lay people, teachers, and professors, encouraged the most able and promising youth to consider the ministry. Persons were urged to commit their lives at an early age. Sometimes these efforts were successful in producing large numbers of ministerial candidates. But they were not always effective in evoking the kind of mature reflection that should inform all decisions to seek ordination. In recent years, almost all Christian churches have lessened their efforts to encourage persons to enter ordained ministry. As a result, many Christians are never invited to consider that they might have such a vocation. A recent survey by the National Opinion Research Center in Chicago reported that 94 percent of Catholic boys between the ages of 14 and adulthood had never even thought about the priesthood for themselves. Similar statistics might well be found for Protestant women and men. Perhaps, in part, the reluctance of the church to lift up its need for ordained ministry is a result of those previous "high pressure" efforts. Also, there is a renewed sensitivity in the church to the fact that authentic ministry is given by God. We tend to wait for candidates to present themselves, trusting that God will raise up ordained ministry for the church.

The right answer is a combination of these positions. We

cannot "recruit" for the ordained ministry; because ministry is not a job among other jobs. It is a "calling." But neither is it necessary, right, or effective to say nothing about ordained ministry, and quietly trust that candidates will come forward. God works in many ways to call persons to ordained ministry. Among these ways is the frank setting forth of the case, challenging able and faithful persons to respond. The church and its leadership is derelict when it fails to do this.

This book makes the case for ordained ministry by looking at its particular nature, role, and work as we move toward the twenty-first century. It is written for all Christians, in an ecumenical context. Consideration is given to the reality of Christian vocation for the whole people of God, and to the nature of the call to ordained ministry from a biblical, historical, and theological point of view. Attention is given to what the church is looking for in its pastors, and to the various questions every person thinking about entering theological education should ask and answer. The nature of the pastoral office, the variety of ways and places in which it can be exercised, and the actual work of the pastor are examined, as are the servant character, moral life, and rewards of ministry. The book ends with the great biblical question: "Who will go for us?" Perhaps through the grace of God and the work of the Holy Spirit you will respond: "Here I am, send me!" (Is. 6:8).

A great deal is at stake. The ordained ministry of the church has a crucial impact on individual lives, and on our common life. Not only the future well-being of the church, but the well-being of the world depends on the leadership rendered by ordained Christian ministers serving in untold ways in every land. I am offering a personal invitation to consider whether you, or someone you know, might be called to serve the church as an ordained minister.

# CHAPTER 1

# Christian Vocation:
# "What Will I Do with My Life?"

*Now there are varieties of gifts, but the same Spirit; and there are varieties of services, but the same Lord; and there are varieties of activities, but it is the same God who activates all of them in everyone. To each is given the manifestation of the Spirit for the common good.*

—1 Corinthians 12:4-7

One of the most important questions every one of us should ask is, "What will I do with my life?" This question is generally thought of as appropriate for high school and college students as they face the future and imagine themselves in a career. From a Christian point of view, however, it is a crucially important question for all of us throughout our lives. Career choice is only one aspect of it. What we do with our lives is seen not just in terms of jobs and careers, but in terms of a total picture of commitment and service.

We live in a time when most people do not put the question in terms of commitment and service. Rather we tend to think of career choice in regard to what we are good at doing, what interests us, or what will make us happy. Even more so, popular articles are written to tell us what jobs will offer the best opportunity to acquire money, power, and things. A dominant concern of many young people today is to get a job that provides high pay, security, and "no risk."

Colleges and universities participate in this way of thinking. Promotional literature, put out to attract students, targets job preparation as a major theme. Universities pride themselves on getting their graduates into law, medical, or business schools. Less attention is given graduate education in the humanities, social sciences, or sciences, perhaps because these are not as lucrative, and therefore not good selling points. Colleges also emphasize their preparation for business and industry, both to meet student demand and as an argument for more public support. Almost all schools have developed programs leading to specific careers, and departments to address questions from students and parents about job preparation. Nothing is inherently wrong with these programs, but they clearly demonstrate that higher education is seen by many as primarily a way of preparing for a career. The leadership of higher education has moved this way to encourage increased spending, and to justify growing costs. Articles documenting higher pay for college graduates appear in the press, offering tangible evidence of the utility of a degree. In a sense, higher education has narrowed its focus and, for reasons having to do with the absence of shared values in both the academy and the society, is now hesitant to address larger questions of character formation which once were understood as part of its role. The traditional arguments for liberal learning sound increasingly antique.

Advertisements from a local men's clothing store near campus in early spring promote "interview suits." The ad promises that purchasing one of these suits will help in the job search, and success will be more likely. Moreover, the store provides free counsel about which shirts and ties should accompany the suit, and offers samples of informal conversation to begin the interview.

The reasons for all of this are not hard to understand. We all participate in it. I know as well as anyone else the pressures on students, parents, indeed on us all, in our economy. It is necessary for us to think about economic realities, and to prepare for the future. At the same time, we need to ask the question, "What are the implications of letting economic considerations become dominant or exclusive?" Several years ago an undergraduate came to see me to talk about problems he was having with his father. The father had a very specific plan in mind for his son. After college he was to go into a corporate training program, then to business school for an MBA, and then into a career in corporate finance. The problem was that the son was not interested in the plan. He had been part of a church-sponsored summer program in Miami working with children at risk. Mature and socially adept, he was effective in public speaking, community organizing, and human relations. He wanted to spend his life trying to effect change in our society's approach to urban problems. To his father this seemed crazy; and the result was serious conflict between them. The father wanted to determine his son's life work and, by doing so, continue his control into adulthood. The son's ideas were not without substance and possibility. He was not proposing that the father support him. There were real jobs that he could do, even if they were not highly lucrative. The son said to me, "My father has one definition of success: making a ton of money and being totally independent."

A college chaplain told me recently that she seldom gets calls from upset parents about how their children are doing in school, either academically or socially. When calls come, they tend to be about a child's religious commitments, especially if they involve serious consideration of mission and service opportunities. They are happy to have a daughter or son involved with campus religious groups as long as those groups do not alter the student's plans. One of the most prevalent areas of conflict between parents and children is what children will do with their lives. The young man who was having trouble with his father was right. At issue is the definition of success. In a time when we talk about "career fast tracks" and "careers with the greatest potential for advancement," it is hard to set forth an alternative way of thinking. At base the issue is the way we consider the meaning of the question, "What will I do with my life?" Recent evidence suggests that our society is recognizing, for the sake of our common good, that we must find a way to call forth renewed commitment to service. Our common life depends on individuals seeing beyond what they perceive to be their own interests to the larger needs of society.

For Christians, the question of what to do with life is more than a matter of career choice, more than money, power, and things, more than security and the absence of risk. Certainly these factors are considered. We would be dishonest to suggest that they can be put aside. We are human beings and participate in the "real world." God entered this "real world" in human form as Jesus Christ and took on these very realities. It is not a matter of ignoring or rejecting material existence. At stake is not letting these realities be the only, or even the most dominant, determinants of our thinking and our acting. The crucifixion and resurrection of Jesus evidence God's truth that the ways of the world are not ultimately decisive. The story of the church in history demonstrates that, in the long run, success cannot be understood only in material terms. This is a fundamental truth that helps to put life into perspective for us all.

During a summer internship in a small town in northern Wisconsin, I visited a sick old man who had spent his whole adult life in that town teaching high school. He was intelligent and cultivated, but a bit depressed. He wondered if he had wasted his life in obscurity without any hint of fame or fortune. About three weeks later he died. At his funeral there were almost two hundred people. One man had come back from New York, where he was a senior officer on the permanent staff of the United Nations. He said to me, "I had to come back to see old Billy off. He was a great man. He opened my eyes to the world and got me to venture forth out of the wilderness of the Northwoods." The achievement of fame and fortune in life is not necessarily related to real success and greatness.

A similar story was told to the *Boston Sunday Globe* on April 5, 1992, by President Nannerl Keohane of Duke University. She went to a little high school in Hot Springs, Arkansas. While there, she had a marvelous teacher: "His name was Bill Mears and he was the first person I had ever known who really challenged me to think in novel ways. *Without him, I would have been different.*" One person, whose life is defined by service and commitment, can have enormous impact for good in ways that are not always immediately evident. Such persons can, and do, make a difference. Thinking of life in ways that go beyond the selfish and material is a major aspect of the concept of Christian vocation.

### What Is Christian Vocation?

One of the greatest insights of the Christian faith is that life must be seen and understood as a whole. We cannot section our lives into what we do to make a living, what we do to have fun, what we do in church, what we do with those we love, what we do for ourselves. These are false separations, even if they are the way we usually think. In the end, our lives only have meaning if they fit together and have significance as a whole. Well-integrated lives are those that hold together all aspects of living so that there is integrity and wholeness. This is why it is a mistake, both conceptually and practically, to separate a job or career from the rest of our activities and involvements.

The idea of Christian vocation is related to the passion for wholeness. The word "vocation" comes from the Latin word *vocare,* which means "to call." Another way of translating it is "to summon." Christians understand themselves to be called, or summoned, by God. God's call comes to all of us. We are called into life itself. Life is given as a gift from God, not as a random happening in a world of chance. We are called to be Christians. Christian faith is a gift from God, not a product of human creation. We are called into the life of the church. The church is a gift from God, not an institution of human origin.

As the body of Christ in the world, the church is called to "stand in" for Christ in the role of servant. The entire ministry of Jesus is described in the New Testament in terms of service. The original Greek word is *diakonia.* The servant role of Jesus became the servant role of the church. In its servant role, the church shares the good news of Jesus Christ, channels God's grace in and to the world, and is a community of active hospitality for all men and women.

It is right to say, therefore, that all Christians have a vocation. Our primary vocation is to be a disciple of Jesus, which means that our professional careers and our personal activities are all subject to the rigors of Jesus' discipline and the power of his promise. Our focus must be on the priority of God's claim on our total life, not just our religious life; because the two cannot meaningfully be separated. From this perspective, there is an almost endless number of jobs in which a Christian can live out his or her vocation. Christian wholeness involves the commitment of one's total life to God, regardless of one's particular work. When Charles

Wesley wrote the great hymn "A Charge to Keep I Have," he intended it for all Christians:

> To serve the present age, my calling to fulfill;
> O may it all my powers engage to do my Master's will.

## What Does It Mean to Say That All Christians Are Ministers?

I received a church bulletin recently from a congregation in New York. I noticed that on the cover, where churches often list the names of staff members, it said, "Ministers: All Members of the Congregation." It then listed the ordained clergy and the lay staff. The point is well made. Through our baptism, Christians become members of the family of God, and part of the church of Jesus Christ. Participation in the church makes us ministers of the gospel, ministers of Christ in the world. This is why you will sometimes hear theologians talk about baptism as a kind of "ordination" to ministry. This language is not without some problems, because it can be confusing about both the theology of baptism and the theology of ordination. Nevertheless, it does suggest an important truth. All Christians are ministers of Jesus Christ.

Since the time of the Protestant Reformation of the sixteenth century, the language of the "priesthood of all believers" has informed Christian thinking. The great German Reformer Martin Luther used this concept to call attention to the shared ministry of all Christians. It certainly was not intended to eliminate or even reduce the importance of an ordained ministry. Luther sought to emphasize the role that all Christians play in the total ministry of the church, and that the whole people of God, both lay and ordained together, constitutes a priestly community.

Sometimes Christians have used the idea of the priesthood of all believers to undercut the clergy, or to endorse an unbridled individualism. In popular terms, individuals can think and do as they please, despite the teachings of the church and its leadership. Many observers, including theologians, sociologists, anthropologists, and historians, have commented on this reality as one of the problems for the teaching authority of the church. But this kind of individualism is not what Luther meant; and it does not represent Christian tradition. No one can be a Christian apart from the community of the church. Every once in a while you will hear people say that this is possible; but it makes no sense. It is a serious misunderstanding of Christian faith. To be a Christian is to be part of a community guided by shared reading of the Scriptures of the Old and New Testaments, and shared expression of Christian tradition. The priesthood of all believers refers to the corporate ministry of the whole community of Jesus Christ; it does not imply a radical individualism, or a lessening of the need for teaching leadership in the church.

In regard to vocation, the priesthood of all believers emphasizes the reality that all Christians are called to live the life of service in their total lives. Thus Christian vocation refers not to a certain group of jobs, such as the pastorate, or other full-time positions of leadership in the church, but to all of the varied roles Christians play in the world. The church must communicate that Christian faith is about total life. There is no possibility of segmenting what we do in the world from what we do in the church. For this reason, the question, "What will I do with my life?" is profoundly important for the Christian. The answer needs to be set in the context of a faithful response to the call of God, through Jesus Christ in the church, to a life lived in relationship to God and the Christian community. In this way it is not only possible, but necessary, to see the incredibly diverse "jobs" Christians do in this world as parts of a total ministry rendered both by individual Christians and by the church as a whole.

People often come to talk with me about their decision to enter seminary to prepare for the professional ministry. In recent years I have been struck by the number who have told me in these interviews that they did not grow up in Christian families, and were never part of the church. In college, university, or in their local communities, they were encountered by Christians who led them to Christ. They began serious Bible study in groups of intentional Christians, and read the Bible for the first time. They became involved in a campus group, or local church, and found the joy and fulfillment of Christian community. They entered into projects of social service in hospitals, schools, prisons, or urban ministries. For many of these new Christians it only seems natural that to be a "real" Christian means going on to seminary. So they present themselves to prepare for "the ministry." I always begin these conversations by getting them to talk about their understanding of the role of the Christian believer, and the role of the ordained minister. Usually they have little or no notion of the idea that all Christians are ministers and contributors to the ministry of the whole community of Jesus Christ. Even more striking, they have no idea whatsoever about what an ordained minister actually does. It is assumed that to be a "real" Christian, one needs to go to seminary and become ordained.

If you have similar perceptions, a word of caution. Certainly it is possible for this kind of call to be genuine, and to lead to a consecrated life of service as a pastor, or some other form of professional minister. But discernment of vocation to ordained ministry takes time; and it is imperative that no one think that it is the only, or even the best, way to live a Christian life. We need to communicate more effectively the need for Christians to serve conscientiously in virtually all walks of life. One's Christian profession does not require moving toward ordination as a pastor. Being a "real" Christian does not mean working for the church in a full-time paid position. Being a "real" Christian is about living life in such a way that the whole is comprehended as Christian vocation. Christian vocation means living a life that becomes the gospel.

Education for the ministry of the church, then, is education for all Christians in Bible, theology, the Christian tradition, and the stories of Christian believers through the years. All Christians need to grow in the faith through serious study, reflection, and prayer; these are not reserved for paid staff of the church, whether laity or clergy. Growing in the faith allows for maturation in understanding Christian vocation. The church celebrates the incredible diversity of gifts for ministry represented in its members. Paul points to this reality in 1 Corinthians 12:4-7:

> Now there are varieties of gifts, but the same Spirit; and there are varieties of services, but the same Lord; and there are varieties of activities, but it is the same God who activates all of them in everyone. To each is given the manifestation of the Spirit for the common good.

God has given these gifts, and it is not desirable that we all be alike or do the same things. What matters is that the defining ambition of our total life is the commitment to service. All Christians are ministers of Jesus Christ in the multiple roles they play in the church and the world.

### Why Should I Consider Ordained Ministry?

The recognition that all Christians are ministers has been emphasized increasingly in the theology of ministry by most churches in recent years. This attention to the ministry of the whole people of God is the result of careful study of understandings of ministry in the Bible, and in the early church. You may wonder, then, why you should consider the ordained ministry. Some members of the church worry that emphasis on all Christians as ministers lessens the importance of the ordained ministry. Is there a correlation between the recognition of the ministry of the whole people of God and a decline in the numbers of persons committing themselves to the ordained ministry? If so, it is because of a misunderstanding about the different roles needed within the church. It is not a matter of either one or the other. The ministry of the whole people of God includes both lay and ordained ministries. Both are given by God, and, as such, are vital and essential to the life of the church. Lay persons desperately want caring, able, and strong pastors to carry out all of the pastoral roles with competence. The laity does not want to displace the ordained ministry.

From the earliest days of the church, some Christians have been set aside for what came to be known as ordained ministry. Throughout this book I will be referring to "ordained ministry" and "ordained ministers." This terminology can be confusing. For one thing, over many generations, most Protestant churches have used the word *minister* in regard to ordained ministers. Usually when we hear that someone is a *minister,* the meaning is what I am calling an "ordained minister." Recent theology of ministry has caused us to be more careful in order to signify the common ministry of all Christians. Terminology is also complicated because different traditions within Christianity use a variety of names: *minister, priest, pastor, rector, preacher.* These titles have tended to indicate a particular role, or emphasis, for the ordained minister within a given tradition. It is even the case that within individual churches a variety of names may be used.

The possibility for confusion does not end with different titles for the pastoral office. It also has to do with differing understandings among the several traditions within world-wide Christianity. Roman Catholic, Orthodox, and Anglican churches, for instance, have three orders of ordained ministers: deacons, presbyters (priests), and bishops. Others, including most of the Protestant churches, have one order of ordained minister (presbyter). United Methodists have two orders (deacons and elders, or presbyters, with elders and bishops understood to hold different offices within the same order). Some churches in the Reformed tradition ordain lay persons for specific functions in the church, even as they set others aside for a permanent ministry of Word and sacrament. Now an important development is new thinking in many churches about the place and role of the deacon, including the office of permanent deacon.

This book is not about the history and theology of these differences or specific offices and orders. It is about the nature of *the call to ordained ministry, the meaning of ordination,* and *the work of the ordained minister.* These can be considered in an ecumenical context, because the ministry of the church of Jesus Christ is a single, shared ministry belonging to no one expression of Christianity. I am using "ordained minister" to refer to a person who is set aside by the church, through the invocation of prayer to the Holy Spirit, and the laying on of hands, for the particular ministries of Word, sacrament, and order. This designation applies to almost all Christian churches and traditions, and is used in regard to persons who serve as pastors in many different roles and settings.

I have tried to use language that suggests the wholeness of what ordained ministry means. This is in keeping with new work in the theology of ministry in most of the churches over at least the last twenty-five years. Therefore, while there are theological differences among the several traditions pertaining to the office and meaning of ordained ministry, for all of them, the call to ordained ministry is about commitment and service to the community of God's people in the ministries of Word and sacrament, and in the ordering of the life of the church for ministry. While the call to ordained ministry is exercised in and through a particular tradition, with its characteristic understandings and emphases, its fundamental character is the same in all Christian communities, because the vocation to ordained ministry is a gift from God.

Ordination is God's gift to the church, and does not belong to any individual; therefore all Christians should be on the lookout for prospective candidates for ordination. Persons are ordained when the church perceives in them gifts and graces for the upbuilding of the community; and specifically for leadership in the ministries of Word, sacrament, and order. The decision about ordination is not an individual one. It is a communal decision involving the candidate and others designated by the church for this purpose. Church members should take seriously their role in the call to ordained ministry and not hesitate to share their sense of another Christian's gifts and graces.

If all Christians should be attentive to those who might be called by God and the church to ordained ministry, so should all Christians be open to the possibility of the call to this ministry. Ordained ministry is necessary for the life of the church. We have not done enough to emphasize our shared responsibility for it. When the question, "What will I do with my life?" is seen as one to be asked within the church, and as one which goes beyond individual preference, to the larger vision of how gifts and talents can be used to serve the good of others, then we are thinking in terms of Christian vocation. This view encourages the church to be on the lookout for persons who might be called for service as pastors.

In the earliest days of the church, leadership was selected and determined by the community according to its perception of who could serve it best. There are many stories about people who tried to avoid selection, but who were commissioned to serve because the church recognized in them the needed gifts and graces. Persons chosen had the ability and capacity to represent the gospel of Jesus Christ, and the witness of the church, to the church and to the wider world. Augustine (AD 354-430), the preeminent thinker, and one of the greatest leaders, of the early church, was ordained unexpectedly and against his intention. Ambrose (AD 340?-397) tried desperately to avoid ordination and service as bishop of Milan. He yielded only because the needs were so great and the people wanted him so badly.

All of us constantly ought to be asking: "What good can I do with my life?" "How can my gifts be used to serve others?" "What is the best thing I can do with my life?" These are not questions just for persons considering ordained ministry. For Christians, the answers to these questions cannot be only about our selfish desires and ambitions, they must be about our sense of service. I talk with a lot of young people, and indeed people of all ages, who are crying out for the opportunity to believe that they are giving their lives for something great. Money, power, and things do not offer meaning or purpose beyond immediate gratification. Christian vocation is the context in which the idea of ordained ministry belongs. Certainly ordained ministry is not the only way for one to live the Christian life of service. But it is one important way that every Christian should consider.

I hope that you will ponder Christian vocation as you ask the question, "What will I do with my life?" All Christians are called to think about their total lives as ministry in the larger ministry of the church. God has need for persons in virtually all occupations, and a sense of the shared ministry should be cultivated. But this attention to the Christian vocation of all Christians does not lessen the importance of ordained leadership. For the sake of the church and the world, there is special need for the vocation to Word, sacrament, and order. Are you sensing God's call to this particular ministry?

# CHAPTER 2

# The Call to Ordained Ministry: "How Do I Know If I'm Called?"

*"Whom shall I send, and who will go for us?" And I said, "Here I am, send me!"*

—Isaiah 6:8

**What Kind of People Is God Looking For?**

In one way or another every ordained minister will attest to having heard the call of God. Perhaps the classic example of call is that of Isaiah. It takes place in the Jerusalem temple after Isaiah experiences God's forgiveness. Having been forgiven and cleansed, Isaiah is free and able to respond to God's call: "Whom shall I send, and who will go for us?" Isaiah becomes a great spokesperson for the Lord. "Who will go for us?" is an abiding question; but it is not necessarily asked in the way it was put to Isaiah. A problem with this classic example is that it has sometimes been taken to be the normative pattern of God's call. While the call of Isaiah is powerful and suggestive, it is not the only way God calls persons to ministry. The call may come in a variety of ways and includes a number of different dimensions. These dimensions are the personal call of God to the individual, the call of God through the church, and the providential call of God.

There are many pastors who can relate dramatic incidents in which God's call to the individual was heard in a personal way with unmistakable clarity. Perhaps it came in a college dorm, in the workplace, or in the quietness of a home or church sanctuary. Such clear calls can literally redirect lives and bring about sharp changes in lifestyle as persons seek to respond. But is also the case that God's call can come in very undramatic ways. If there are many who point to a specific time and place when God's call was heard, there are just as many who talk about the gradual development of a sense of God's call. Sometimes this kind of call takes months or years of growth to come to focus. It is neither helpful nor accurate to think that there is only one way in which God calls persons into ordained ministry. Usually persons talk of this call coming in a highly personal way, including the immediate experience of God wanting one to explore ordained ministry. But the individual experience must be confirmed by the community. Discerning the call involves relating the personal call to the call of the church.

In addition to the call of God to the individual, ordained ministers have heard the call of the church. It may have come from a pastor, a Sunday School teacher, a college professor, a chaplain, or an astute fellow worker in the local congregation: "I think you have the gifts and graces for the ordained ministry of the church; have you considered it?" The call of the church also involves steps in which vocation is recognized and confirmed through a long and complex process of education, spiritual formation, pastoral supervision, and examination. Sometimes the phrase "ecclesiastical" call is used. Although it is unintended, that phrase can sound too institutional. The call of the church is not primarily about being granted credentials or organizational authorization. It has to do with the role of the Christian community in lifting up leadership for its own good. It is the communal call to ordained ministry.

At a retreat for ministerial candidates I noticed one young man who was obviously not a participant. He sat silent and alone at the edge of the group. His appearance evidenced an arrogance that distanced him from me and the others who were seriously engaged in the proceedings. Finally during one of the open discussion sessions, he could not contain himself any longer. He spoke up saying that he resented the whole experience. "I don't like having to be at this retreat, and I don't like having my call from God tested and evaluated." He was convinced that he was called to preach, and therefore he should be allowed to do so. The multiple requirements of the church seemed to him like an endless series of high hurdles to be jumped in the race toward ordination. He judged the whole process to be excessive, inappropriate, and perhaps contrary to God's will. The anxiety that attends all evaluation soured him on the retreat because it was a required part of the process. But his interjection was helpful. He expressed feelings we all have at times. Some of his tension was released; and the outburst occasioned a lengthy discussion about the complex nature of call, especially in regard to the role of the church.

Many of us know people who assert that they have been called by God into the ordained ministry but have not been approved for ordination and service as a pastor. Usually we can see good reasons for the church's decision. A long-experienced pastor's widow, Estelle Hillman, who was herself a formidable leader and astute judge of the clergy, once was talking to me about a young man who wanted to be ordained. "He says it's a call from God," she remarked, "but I think it's from his grandmother." There is, and always must be, a balance between our conviction of God's call and our recognition and acceptance of the church's call. Both need to be present.

The view expressed by the young candidate at the retreat is not unusual. Many people think that the church, because it is a community of compassion, should never turn anyone down. Ordained ministry, however, is the church's ministry; it belongs to no individual. From its earliest days, the church has had processes for identifying and approving ordained leadership. These processes have taken different forms throughout history because times and needs differ. The qualifications for ordained ministry and expectations of the churches have changed with the times as well. Some examination, evaluation, and affirmation on the part of the people of God, however, has always been required for authorized ministry in the community of Jesus Christ.

The personal call of God to the individual and the call of the church go together, and should be understood as compatible. Even so, although they are complementary, one or the other may be experienced first. A student preparing for the ordained ministry told me that it had never occurred to her that she might be a pastor. She was actively involved as a lay person in a particular congregation. One evening after a churchwide supper at which she had made a presentation, an older man in the congregation asked her if she had ever thought that God might be calling her into ordained ministry. "It was like a light bulb coming on in my head," she said. "From that moment forward I couldn't stop thinking about his question." She asked her pastor to meet with her to evaluate her gifts and graces, and he enthusiastically agreed that she was equipped for the call. It was then that she began a systematic effort to discern whether she was experiencing God's call. With her pastor's help she sought further confirmation from the congregation. She prayed for guidance and studied the Scriptures to ponder the way God raises up leadership. She is now in seminary because of a strategic spontaneous question from a lay person in her local church. He was attentive to the need of the church, and his suggestion opened the door for her to hear God's call.

If there is any need to offer justification for the church confronting people with the possibility of ordained ministry, stories like this are instructive. I remember vividly going to a church youth conference with my pastor when I was fourteen years old. Bishop Charles Wesley Brashares was presiding, and one portion of the conference was given to an invitation to those gathered to consider "the call to preach." In an eloquent, simple, and moving statement, the bishop challenged us to give prayerful thought to the possibility that we might be called to the ministry of the church. Later in the day I happened to encounter him in the hallway. He stopped and shook my hand, remembering that he had met me once before. Looking me directly in the eye (he was a short, old man at the time, talking to a boy of fourteen), he said, "Dennis, I want you to be a minister; and I want you to go to Boston." His reference was to Boston University, his own school, and the school of many Methodist bishops in those days. I honored half of his request; I did not end up at Boston, though his commitment to his *alma mater* was commendable. The impression that encounter made on me was powerful. It made me think seriously about the ordained ministry. It planted a seed which germinated years later. None of us should underestimate the importance of reminding others of the greatness of the call to ordained ministry and that someone cares that we think about it.

Sometimes you will hear it said that we should not "recruit" for the ministry because it is a "calling." All Christians are called by God to faith in Jesus Christ. Some are also called by God for the particular ministry of ordained leadership through a personal call to the individual and a public call from the church. These go together; both are necessary; but they may come separately; and one is not necessarily prior to the other. Certainly we should not "recruit" for ordained ministry as if it were a job among other jobs. But we must let Christians know that God calls people to ordained ministry in and through the church, and that they should be attentive and open to the call.

When you hear people say that the call of the church is "not enough," they mean that no one should enter the ordained ministry without a strong personal sense of God's call. This is surely right. But it is also the case that no one should enter the ordained ministry without a sure sense of the call of the church. We all can be blind to certain realities about ourselves. The church may see in us gifts and graces we do not see. Similarly the church may see problems and liabilities we do not see. There is a complementarity about the various aspects of the call. Though there may be anxiety during the time of discernment, in due season an experience of quiet certainty offers resolution. The reality of the call needs to be kept alive, however. The call of God to ordained ministry is not settled once and for all. I often heard the late United Methodist Bishop W. Kenneth Goodson say that whenever he was asked the inevitable question, "When were you called to preach?" his answer was, "The last time was this morning." He went on to assert that if one did not have the urgent sense of call, then some hard questions needed to be asked. An abiding and immediate sense of call is necessary for authentic and effective ministry. The reality of God's call is dynamic; it is not something that takes place only once at a given time. It continues to undergird ministry with a sense of the rightness of the work.

In addition to the call of God to the individual, and the call of the church, there is also what may be called the "providential call." By this we mean the gifts of God for ministry that allow a person not only to hear but also to respond with effectiveness. In the next section I will discuss some of the specific gifts which need to be present for response to the call. Ideally the various aspects of call all go together. What we are able to do, what we like to do, and what we are good at doing should come together with what God and the church want us to do. They do not always; and the challenge is to recognize that sometimes our own wills and preferences need to be adjusted for the sake of God and the church.

What kind of people is God looking for? God is looking for persons who are sensitive to the possibility that their gifts and graces, their total lives, might be shaped in such a way as to be used for the service of God's people. God is looking for bright and able people who can bring to the ordained ministry deep commitment to spread the gospel. God is looking for persons who will say, with humility and enthusiasm, "Here I am, send me."

### What Kind of People Is the Church Looking For?

The answer to the question of what kind of people the church is looking for is not simple. The churches are seeking a significant diversity of persons because there is a significant diversity of ministerial needs. Church history shows that God and the church have used an amazingly wide variety of persons for leadership, and that the qualifications for ordination, and the expectations of the churches, have varied through the years. God can work in and through some people who at first are viewed as very unlikely both in the eyes of the church and in the eyes of the world. All Christians should ponder the possibility that they might be called to ordained ministry, and we should be careful not to discourage any thoughtful consideration. It is finally up to the church to determine suitability for its ordained ministry, and this suitability can be ascertained only after prayerful examination and testing. Nevertheless, there are some qualifications which are enduring. Reflection on these will be of help to persons thinking about the call to ordained ministry.

**The church is looking for people of deep faith and personal commitment to Jesus Christ.** Seriousness about the spiritual life must come first. I do not mean that only those well along the path to spiritual maturity should consider ordained ministry. That would eliminate most ordained ministers. The notion that ordained ministers are necessarily more spiritually mature than other Christians is inaccurate. Almost every congregation has within it persons whose own spiritual development is such that it puts the clergy to shame. Nor do I mean that persons considering ordained ministry should have no doubts or uncertainties. The church is looking for persons who are committed to Christ, and who understand that they constantly must work at their own spiritual formation so that they can be in ministry with others. The spiritual growth which comes from the disciplined life of prayer and Scripture study is essential to discerning the call to ordained ministry, to sustaining the call through years of preparation, and to keeping the call alive in diverse and difficult ministry settings. Spiritual seriousness requires willingness to work for growth in faith; and it involves commitment to a schedule that includes time for quiet contemplation every day.

Personal prayer and contemplation do not take the place of corporate worship, of course. Corporate worship is the most important work of the Christian community. It is where the community places itself before God and is reminded of its role as God's people in the world. Strong commitment to both individual worship and corporate worship is necessary for the ordained minister. These essential opportunities relate us to God, contribute to faith development, and provide continuing spiritual strength for ministry. The work of worship never stops for the ordained minister because it keeps the gift of ministry alive. "Hence I remind you to rekindle the gift of God that is within you through the laying on of my hands" (2 Tim. 1:6).

**The church is looking for people who have gifts for intellectual development and a concern for learning.** The ordained ministry requires a willingness and ability to study and learn throughout one's life. The degree of learning varies, of course. Not all ordained ministers need to be educated to the same degree, any more than they need to be the same in any other way. But all need to have a passion for knowing as much as they can about the Bible, the Christian tradition, the history of the church, the various disciplines involved in preaching, worship and pastoral care, and the world in which the people they serve live. This is not the place to discuss in detail the wide range of knowledge and skills a competent ordained minister ought to have. But the church is looking for people who will take upon themselves the responsibility of learning in order that they can lead the rest of the church to grow in faith.

When talking with lay people, especially those in congregations where our students do their internships, they will often say things to me that they will not say to their pastor or to a ministerial student. I am struck by their concern for the teaching ministry. Churches want their pastor to have a thorough knowledge and understanding of the Bible, and to be able to teach it to the children, youth, and adults. They want their pastor to think theologically so that pastoral problems, and even the administrative problems of the church, can be put in a theological context. They want their pastor to know about the world and be knowledgeable about the variety of issues appropriate to their given ministry setting. Included among these issues is some real understanding of the context in which their people live, and the kinds of work they do. They do not ever want to be embarrassed by their pastor's ignorance in a world where the people of God are ever more well-educated.

Persons preparing for ordained ministry sometimes complain about the amount of study required. I remind students that they are incredibly privileged. They are given the opportunity and freedom to spend their days and nights in study and preparation while most Christians are less free to devote time for reflection. Throughout history the church has set aside some of its members for study so that they could learn the Christian tradition and pass it on. Educational preparation for ordained ministry is itself a corporate reality. It is not the education of an individual just for the sake of that person; seen rightly, it is education for the sake of the church. One of the major roles of the ordained minister is to teach and interpret the Christian Scriptures and the apostolic faith with faithfulness, integrity, care, and effectiveness. The teaching role is not just to pass on inherited knowledge, though that is important, but also to help others learn to think theologically and to share their understanding of the Christian gospel in daily life. Ordained ministers are charged with acquiring special knowledge and expertise, and their competence, or lack of it, is readily recognized by the laity.

**The church is looking for people who have the ability and commitment to apply their learning to the actual work of ordained ministry.** It is not enough to have the gift for learning, or acquired knowledge. An ordained minister must be passionately committed to applying what has been learned to the needs of congregations in actual ministry settings. It is easy to have an image of the "ideal" church or "model" Christian community. The challenge is to see the power and reality of the gospel of Jesus Christ in the most unlikely and imperfect places where God's people are nevertheless gathered. Ordained ministers need the ability and will to develop practical skills of application. These do not come automatically, and there are a number of them that require particular attention.

It is essential that ordained ministers be gifted communicators. Communication involves the exacting work of effective speaking and writing. All the knowledge in the world about Christianity will do no good if the one who has it is unable to communicate it to everyday people. Some persons are naturally gifted communicators, able to speak and write with ease. Others must work very hard to develop these skills. Every one of us needs to improve, however; and communication skills can be learned and perpetually enhanced. The churches are looking for leaders who are good communicators. Without question, lay persons most often ask that we "teach them to preach." The church wants preachers who can communicate the nature and meaning of the Christian faith in such a way that the power of the gospel to change lives is made real. There is no greater opportunity or responsibility than entering the pulpit to preach the Word of God.

Another urgent need of the church is for pastors who know what leadership is about and are willing and eager to play this role. The purpose of ordained ministry is to provide leadership for the community of Jesus Christ. This is the reason the church sets some of its members aside as ordained ministers. Without leadership it cannot exist as a community. Leadership requires willingness to contribute to shaping the community in a way consistent with the gospel, and to see everything that is done by the pastor in the community as judged by the intention of Christian faith. It implies a confidence that one knows what to do and how to do the work expected by the church. It also implies a creative ability not to let the expected work be so draining that there is no larger vision.

The ability and willingness to apply the knowledge required for ministry takes courage. Communication of the gospel and leadership in the church community is not easy, nor is the maintenance of identity and integrity when one ministers in the larger community beyond the church. One mistake can be to use knowledge and experience as weapons to attack those who disagree, another is to wither at the first sign of opposition. A pastor must be willing to learn to balance confidence with flexibility while not falling into rigidity or weakness. Positive response to God's call to ordained ministry implies a commitment to develop the necessary skills to put knowledge into practice.

**The church is looking for people who have a genuine love of people, an outgoing personality, and developed relational skills.** These qualities may seem obvious requirements for ordained ministers, but sometimes the obvious is missed. I know well a man who entered ordained ministry because he had strong ideas about the church and wanted to shape it to conform to his ideal vision. The trouble was that the people he sought to serve also had ideas, some of which they were not willing to give up. He ran into constant problems because he could not bring his vision to reality in a short time. In talking with him I was struck by his references to his parishioners. They were "dumb," "stubborn," "set-in-their-ways"; I got no sense from him that he could simply enjoy them as people. There was no appreciation for the fact that they had other interests besides his, no capacity to relax and find possibilities for ministry in occasions that did not involve study or social action. He was ambitious and goal oriented in everything; but he did not exhibit the heart of a pastor that allows one to recognize the value and integrity of people different from oneself. A pastor's heart brings forth sensitivity and empathy. It allows one to keep perspective and not lose sight of the fact that the ordained minister does not have all the answers.

The privilege of ordained ministry can be misused. There is potential for manipulation of people; and the authority and influence of the pastorate can be made to serve the goal of self-gratification. The role of the ordained minister has the potential for harm if it is exercised by a rigid person seeking to control others, or a weak person seeking any number of kinds of self-gratification. If one honestly seeks to serve, then a fundamental respect for persons and appreciation of them, as they are, is necessary before one can help them shape their lives into a community of Christ. The pastor needs to be able to recognize and evoke the best in people.

Although the church can and does use a wide diversity of people in ordained ministry, the four general qualifications I have mentioned above are essential. No one combines these qualities in the same way; and, through the gift of the Holy Spirit, they can be developed and enhanced in a person willing to respond to God's call. Even if all of the essential qualities are present; and even if there is potential to develop specific skills and abilities, there remains another important question that must be asked: "Are you willing to allow your own will and desires to be shaped to meet the needs of the life of the community of Jesus Christ?" All of the qualities I have noted as essential may be present in a person, and yet the will to allow them to be used for Christ's people may not be there. God needs persons who will respond to this great challenge. It is easy to use our talents simply to suit ourselves; but, although it is harder, it is far more significant to use them in ways that serve others. An ordained minister must be willing and committed to enhance his or her talents and abilities so that they will be in accord with the needs of the church.

## The Shaping of Servant Identity

Most of us do not like to adjust our own interests to conform to the needs and desires of others. One of the things we must learn as children is that we cannot always get our own way. As we mature, we develop ways of relating to other people so that there is an equilibrium between what we want to be and do, and what we are able to do in relationship to others. Some persons never learn to accommodate others. Central to the call to ordained ministry is the recognition that acceptance of the call involves a willingness to let the church participate in the shaping of the self. It does not mean a total relinquishment of the self; such an idea is both impossible and unhealthy. The church needs pastors who have strong self-images and real ego strengths. At the same time, effectiveness as an ordained minister requires the surrender of an attitude of singular self-will. One way of thinking about this is with the biblical image of servant. All Christians are called to be servants; the ordained minister is called to be servant of servants.

The reality of the role of servant of servants is one of the most important considerations for anyone thinking about the ordained ministry. No one is forced into ordained ministry. It is one of the greatest gifts from God that can be given; but, like other gifts, it can be accepted with thanks, or rejected. If it is accepted, it involves some relinquishment of the self for the sake of service.

A student had completed his summer field education in a small-membership church in a rural area and wanted to talk. The experience had been good; but in the course of the twelve weeks, he had determined that he did not want to continue on the path to ordination. His reasons were almost exclusively concerned with the matter of identity. He perceived, correctly I thought, that he had all the personal qualities and gifts to be effective in ministry; but he did not like the fact that the church cared about his private life. He told me that he felt as though he were expected to live without privacy. In a small town, a ministerial intern cannot live in anonymity. It does not take long for the whole community to know that a new student pastor is in town. They were interested in what he did with "his time off" and with whom he and his wife were friends. The "public" nature of the ministry bothered him. He preferred having total privacy and doing exactly what he wanted when he wanted. I assured him that these kinds of concerns frequently arise as persons consider ordained ministry. In fact, as we will see later in this book, there are good reasons for this. The nature of ordained ministry includes a "representative character" which makes these questions inevitable; and they are not all bad, although one must come to terms with the privileges and demands of ministerial identity.

Sometimes there are seriously inappropriate efforts on the part of parishioners to control the lives of pastors and, perhaps, pastor's families. There are stories of parsonage committees, church boards, and even individuals getting out of hand in their efforts to exert control, intrude on privacy, and impose unrealistic or unfair expectations. But such incidents need not undermine ministry if the pastor understands the dynamic of congregational life, and balances firmness with pastoral sensitivity, while keeping communication open.

Ordained ministry involves a relationship with the church in which one's identity is shaped by the church. This is, or should be, true of all Christians. It is true of pastors in a special and particular way. One of the realities of ordained ministry is that everything bears on the role. To put it another way, one does not work for eight hours and then stop being an ordained minister. This does not mean that work never stops; but it means that one never ceases to represent Christ and the church. This representative role cannot be turned off at the end of a work day. By definition, the ordained minister is a personal representative of the Christian community.

Servant identity means that one is willing to accept this kind of role. It is possible to be enormously talented, and to have all of the abilities to be an effective ordained minister, and yet be ineffective. What is missing is the willingness to give of the self for the good of the church and the world. At root of servant identity requires sufficient spiritual depth and maturity to permit the sharing of one's individuality with a community. This is not easy. Many times the demands of the church are frustrating. The recognition of servanthood provides perspective, and permits insights about how frustration can be constructive so that it is not paralyzing. Servant identity transforms persons in such a way that they are shaped for God's work in the world. It allows one to be freed from undue preoccupation with the self for the sake of others. In the case of married pastors, servant identity can also be a gift to the family. Usually the total attitude of the pastor will influence that of a spouse and children. The conviction that the family has more to worry about than its own selfish desires and ends is a powerful witness for Christ, and a contributor to family solidarity. When servant identity is accepted with understanding and appreciation, it is one of the great gifts of ordained ministry.

## Six Specific Questions

*1. What about "seekers" in seminary?* What about the person, the seeker, who has a definite interest in the ordained ministry, but is genuinely uncertain about the call? Is there a place in theological education for the person who is not sure of vocation but who wants to explore both the Christian faith and the possibility of a calling to ministry? Of course! Seekers are invited to explore ministry, and are welcome in theological schools. At the same time, if you are such a person, there are circumstances to be considered.

Seekers must understand that the curriculum of the theological school is established to educate persons for the lay and ordained ministries of the church. One of the best ways of exploring ministry is by entering into a curriculum with commitment and enthusiasm. One cannot expect the school to alter its curriculum to accommodate seekers. A student complained bitterly that he had to take a required course. He argued that it did not apply to him, and did not meet his needs, because he was not certain that he was going to be a professional minister, whether lay or ordained. I suggested to him that he would never know unless he was tested in the kind of courses required in the curriculum. Furthermore, a theological school is a professional school in the sense that it exists to help prepare persons for the church's ministry. If he simply wanted to take courses in religion, there were ways it could be done through graduate programs in the liberal arts.

Theological education requires participation in actual communities of faith as one learns leadership in the church. Seekers ought to understand the expectations and legitimate claims of both the school and the churches. Neither exists for the self-interests of individuals. Seekers are welcome in theological education, if they are serious, open, and ready to participate fully in the life and work of the theological school in all of its dimensions. Seekers also need to be committed to growing in Christian faith and in spiritual depth, as they discern the nature of their own vocation. One can only assess call and response in the context of the excitement generated through lively engagement with the issues of ministry.

*2. What age is right?* The call to ordained ministry may come to a person at any age. I do not know why God calls persons at such different stages of life; but the evidence is clear that persons of all ages are called, and that persons of all ages can be effective in ministry. Not too many years ago it was common in all of the churches for persons to enter the ordained ministry when they were young, and serve for forty or more years. The normal pattern was to enter a seminary after college graduation and then take up service in the church. The model was that of the other professions, and the image was that of a career. In recent years there has been a change in virtually all of the churches. More and more persons are called into ordained ministry out of other careers. Theological schools now have large numbers of students who previously worked in jobs, or served in professions, of every conceivable kind. The average age of students in Christian theological schools in almost all parts of the world has risen steadily over the past twenty-five years. As a result, seminary student bodies have a wide range of ages represented within them.

What kind of consideration should a person thinking about the call to ordained ministry give to age? Age is no deterrent to effectiveness as a student, or to fine service as a pastor. Nevertheless, some thought should be given to the length of time one can reasonably serve. Churches know that theological education and preparation for ordained ministry are expensive; and the length of time that one can serve is a legitimate issue. As in any work that matters, experience contributes to effectiveness. The experience that is brought by persons from other occupations to the ordained ministry has enhanced the church; and skills developed in business, industry, or the professions can translate well into church leadership.

It is especially important for younger persons not to think that the call to ordained ministry normally comes to those who are already established in other careers. The opening up of seminary education to older persons is to be celebrated; but it does not follow that younger persons do not belong in theological education. Younger students are often the most open and enthusiastic about the challenges of theological study because they are not in so much of a hurry to finish and begin the actual practice of ministry. Persons in college or university should be open to the call of God and the call of the church. Many great leaders of the church first saw the vision of a life of significant service in ordained ministry when it was put before them while they were still in high school or college.

The church hungers for young people of faith to respond to the invitation to consider the church's ministry. There are some roles that can be filled unusually well by young pastors. One of these is in youth and student ministries, working with young people who face increasingly difficult problems in contemporary society. Another is initiating and building new congregations of faithful disciples of Jesus Christ. A third is social ministries in urban or rural mission settings, where hope is almost extinguished; and the vitality and energy of the young pastor can be transformative. Persons who accept the call to ordained ministry at a young age have the opportunity to serve in a wide variety of settings over many years, or to develop particular expertise in a special area of need and remain within it. The experience that comes from long years of service is vital for seasoned leadership in the church and in the society beyond the Christian community. The challenge to young people today is to imagine themselves moving into ordained ministry after college and taking upon themselves the yoke of service to God throughout a lifetime of ministry.

3. *What education is expected?* As with many of the questions associated with ministry, there is no easy answer to this question. In most North American churches, and in the case of most persons called to ministry, the normal expectation is

that one will complete a four-year baccalaureate degree in an approved college or university, and also a program of theological education. This graduate-professional theological education, alternatively called seminary, follows undergraduate education, and generally involves three or four years of study and internship.

In some churches only approved candidates may enter seminary. These approved candidates will already have satisfied the church about their spiritual seriousness and their willingness to grow in the faith. There is a mutual obligation between the church and the candidate once a person begins the journey. The good thing about this model is that the church starts to take responsibility for the nurturing of candidates for ordination even before theological education begins. Prior to entering seminary a candidate is evaluated in regard to spiritual readiness; and the subsequent formation that goes on in seminary can be shaped according to the expectations of the church. The church thus lends guidance and support throughout the course of preparation. This approach to theological education is characteristic of the Roman Catholic, Orthodox, Episcopal, and Lutheran churches in particular, though the Presbyterian and Methodist churches also have similar procedures for candidacy. Some of the smaller churches, especially those that have only a few seminaries, may be more specific about requiring students who are under the care of the church, and who are clearly moving toward ordination, to follow precise programs in designated schools. It should be emphasized, however, that in virtually none of the churches is the process airtight. Often persons start theological education and then initiate candidacy by coming under the care of a bishop, a conference, a synod, or some other official church body. Also, it is not uncommon for ministerial students to change churches, or to move into different relationships with churches, in the course of seminary.

Within Christianity there are many kinds of theological schools. Even the terminology is diverse. There are "seminaries," "theological schools," "divinity schools," "schools of theology," "Bible schools," and "schools of religion." These terminological variables are the product of different churches, different theological traditions, and different understandings about the nature and place of theological education. The relationship of theological education to higher education, in general, and to other institutions of higher education, in particular, is one of the key issues that differentiate churches.

For some traditions, entry into ordained ministry has almost always required a prescribed program of theological education. The Roman Catholic Church, the Orthodox churches, the Lutheran churches, and the Episcopal (or Anglican) churches have generally mandated a full seminary course of study prior to ordination. Moreover, the requirement, or at least the preference, was for persons to attend seminaries run by these churches. The United Church of Christ (Congregational churches) and the Presbyterian churches also have a tradition of an educated ministry, although they have usually been more open to candidates with degrees from a wide variety of theological schools, including those that are part of universities. Methodists were later to come to the idea that education in a school of theology should be expected; and while Methodism has an outstanding group of theological schools, Methodists have usually received pastors from many different approved schools. Baptists, because of their strong sense of congregational independence, have never had common denominational educational requirements, although Baptist seminaries, and other theological schools, educate a large number of Baptist pastors. Many pastors in the free church tradition are educated in independent Bible schools.

The wide variety of theological schools can be a source of confusion. There are some theological schools supported by specific churches which primarily educate persons for those denominations, some schools related to churches which have quite denominationally diverse student bodies, and some schools which officially declare themselves as "nondenominational," and which have students from many different traditions. Increasingly, in many churches, there is a recognition that some ecumenical experience and training is valuable; and programs of study in a particular tradition are often enhanced with exposure to other Christian traditions. University centers of theological education provide one way of achieving this aim. Centers for training in particular denominational traditions can coincide with ecumenical faculties, research libraries, and shared educational facilities.

Theological schools differ not only denominationally, but also in regard to their structures. There are schools that are part of universities, in the same way that a law school is part of a university; there are free-standing theological schools, which are not part of a university, but which have an educational relationship to a college, university, or another seminary, or group of seminaries; and there are schools with no relationship to a university, or other institution of higher education. The reason for this is that among most of the churches in America, there never was only one way to prepare for ministry. An incredible diversity of options therefore grew up in the freedom of American Christianity.

Sometimes students respond to the call to ministry by choosing a school and then, when they near the completion of their degree, seek a church in which to be ordained. This pattern conforms to a twentieth-century model of professional education for law and medicine in which students are accepted by a school, complete a course of study, and then seek acceptance into the profession. This is a problematic approach to theological education for both theological and practical reasons. Theologically, we understand ordained ministry as a communal reality. It is not just an individual decision. It is reached in the context of the church's ministry. Practically, it is difficult, and inappropriate, for a church to accept a candidate for ordination simply because the person arrives having completed a theological degree.

Persons considering the ordained ministry should not be confused or frustrated by these historical and theological diversities. The best advice is to start by seeking counsel from a pastor, chaplain, teacher, or other church leader. It is often wise to talk to a number of persons, because advice can differ; and not all advisors are equally up-to-date. It is particularly important to talk with someone who can provide a sense of the larger issues, and not just personal opinion. Most theological educators advise that anyone seriously considering entry into a theological school learn as much as possible about the expectations and procedures of his or her church before entering a program of study. No one should move forward without seeking broad advice and visiting a number of different schools. Avoid facile generalizations and simple answers. Especially beware of those who undercut the importance of education, or propose to offer easier routes through extension programs, correspondence courses, or congregationally-based initiatives. Ordained ministry is too important to think that there are short cuts. Such ideas serve neither the candidate nor the churches. The development of servant identity for ministry requires communal involvement in classrooms, chapel, library, and formation groups. There are no easy answers about theological education; and prospective students should beware of advisors who think it is simple, or that only one way is right.

*4. What about finances?* The financial aspects of theological education require thoughtful and prayerful attention. No financial situation is impossible. Theological education can be achieved, but the realities of income and expense deserve careful planning. For a young, unmarried person the problems are obviously less complex than for a person who is married, or who has children; but financial concerns are almost universal.

The church cannot assume total responsibility for those preparing for ministry. Occasionally one comes across a seminary application in which it appears that a candidate is looking to the church more as an answer to problems than as an opportunity to serve. This is a mistake; and it is neither fair nor wise to think that the church has either obligation or capacity to deal with a student's financial difficulties. No person should begin theological education without a plan that sets out clearly how financial obligations will be managed in order to avoid large indebtedness. American higher education today is built on the assumption that most students will incur a certain amount of indebtedness. Loans are taken out for undergraduate and graduate education, and then they are paid back during the early earning years. In some professions, such as law, this model is well-established. The higher incomes now expected by young attorneys are directly related to the need to pay back what are often very large educational loans. Most theological students probably will take on some indebtedness; but the relatively low salaries paid to pastors in the years following seminary will not permit repayment of large loans without severe strain. The answer is not discouragement, but planning.

Several years ago a student arrived unannounced to begin divinity school. He came without resources and planned to pitch a tent in which to live. (I am not making this up.) He was something of a rustic; but still, there was no place for his tent on the campus. It was his conviction that he was called to preach; and that the Lord would provide, if only he started out, and then followed God's lead. At least he had no wife or children. Some persons show up with whole families in tow expecting that the school would take them under its wing, and that finances would take care of themselves. Finances never take care of themselves.

The kind of responsibility required for financial planning is the same kind of responsibility required for effective service. You should not hesitate to consider ordained ministry because of financial worry. But if the call is authentic, it will not go away; and there will be time to get the financial plan accomplished. Starting seminary without a financial plan is never wise. At the same time, my advice to prospective students is that the sooner you get started, the better. Here younger students do have an advantage. It is more complicated to begin seminary after one has the increased financial obligations that almost inevitably come with growing older. The joys and opportunities of ministry in the church of Jesus Christ are so great that financial issues should not, and need not, finally stand in the way. At the same time, they take time to work out; and the time given is well-spent.

5. *How will my family deal with this?* Most parents, brothers and sisters, spouses, and children are delighted and enthusiastic about a person entering the ministry. For many parents the call of a child to ordained ministry is an answer to prayer. Sometimes persons who experience the call to ordained ministry find their families opposed. If so, an additional dimension is added to one's consideration. Family negativity may be the result of perceptions about the professional ministry held by some persons in the church and in the general society.

A chief reservation may have to do with the status of the ministry. At one time in American culture the ordained ministry ranked high in the social order in terms of respect and power. This was so because the church itself was a dominant institution. Now, as a result of movement toward a more secular society, and greater diversity resulting from increased cultural pluralism, the role and place of the church in American society is changing. Some people think that the church is not as dominant a reality in the United States as it once was. If this is true, then the ordained leadership of the church is in a less central role in the social order; and therefore the status associated with the ministry is not as great as in previous generations. It should be emphasized that this sociological point of view is by no means the only consideration. There are important theological considerations about the reality of ordained ministry that are more important. Nevertheless, the changed social location of the ministry means that clergy are not necessarily, or automatically, in a commanding role in the larger society. For this reason, some family members, perhaps especially parents, may object to one thinking about ministry.

Directly related to status and social location is the matter of money. Ordained ministers are not "paid for their work" as though they were employees. Instead, the Christian community provides them with support to set them free for service. Family members may regret that a child or spouse does not seek a high-paying occupation. Often parents, in particular, will express the view that, given the amount of expensive education involved in preparation for ordained ministry, the salaries should be greater. This is not, and cannot be, the way to think about ordained ministry and money; nevertheless money is often a factor that affects family reaction. Some parents are concerned about what their children do, and how much money they make, because of how it reflects on them. Their own status is enhanced by what their son or daughter does, and how much money goes with it.

A third factor in family reaction has to do with the lifestyle of the ordained minister, and especially the issues of privacy and freedom. Lifestyle can be a major cause of negative reaction on the part of a spouse, or child, in the case of older persons considering ministry. A family's privacy is affected because the ministry is a representative public role. The pastor's family is inevitably related to the congregation, and to the entire ministry. There is also a lessening of freedom because ordained ministry is not an eight-hour-a-day job. Pastoral needs of members of the congregation do not stop at the end of the day, and calls come continually. Obviously there are ways to limit demands; clergy cannot and should not be always and immediately available. Most congregations understand that pastors and their families need uninterrupted leisure. Nevertheless, there are times when a pastor must go, regardless of the hour of the day or night. This, in fact, is one of the greatest opportunities of the ministry. Some service is unique and can be done only by the ordained minister. There are times when pastoral demands require that long-established plans be changed.

Although the three reasons for family objection mentioned above are the most common, there are others which should be noted. These include the unpredictability of where one might serve as a pastor, the possibility that clergy housing might be restrictive, or that the church is filled with hypocrites playing "politics." There is no way to answer all of these objections to satisfy some family critics. This is so because the objections are based on a way of thinking that is not rightly applicable to ministry, whether lay or ordained. All of the objections grow out of a worldview that puts selfish interests in the first place. These human desires for status, money, comfort, pleasure, or independence are compelling; we cannot banish them from our experience, even if we try. As Christians, however, we are challenged to orient our lives in such a way that our call to service (the *diakonia* of Jesus) comes first. The objections to ordained ministry cannot be answered if the standard used is that of secular ambition and acquisition. Ministry requires a different standard; we are invited to look at life from the point of view of God's call to service in Jesus Christ.

It is nevertheless important to work through family objections. They can be serious; and they deserve attention. In the case of parents, the problem is more manageable because, in the end, every one of us must break from the control of mother and father. Parents may object to any number of vocations; and we cannot let their objections determine or limit our lives. Even if parents seek to discourage answering the call, they will be sympathetic if they come to understand the larger dimensions, including the real power, of the call to ordained ministry. A parental objection can provide a growing experience and a testing of our own perceptions. If they are willing, it is often helpful for parents to meet with a pastor, or another lay person, to talk about their feelings.

The more serious objections are those that come from a spouse. In the case of a person who is considering the invitation to ordained ministry after having been married, the decision is more complex. A spouse, after all, did not bargain for years of seminary preparation and a life in direct relation to pastoral ministry. The age of the person called, as well as those of a spouse and children, makes a significant difference. A change in the role and identity of one partner affects the other. A physical move, different work, and change of lifestyle may be required. If a spouse is reluctant but open, then thoughtful counsel with a pastor, bishop, seminary dean or professor, or other counselor, along with prayer and conversation, may bring assurance that ordained ministry can be a marvelous gift to a family. If, however, the objections are serious and deeply felt, it is important to spend a great deal of time thinking, talking, and praying. It is never wise to go ahead over strong objections on the part of a spouse. Indeed it could be argued that in such a case the call may be misinterpreted. God's call to ordained ministry is probably not authentic if it results in a spouse being confused and unhappy. It is crucial at this point to emphasize the call of the church. The Christian community can be both a support and a guide when there is family objection to one of its members answering a call to ordained ministry.

6. *Might my talents be used more effectively for God in a more powerful profession?* Almost inevitably, bright and talented young people ask this question about ordained ministry. Many think that their impact on the world of affairs might be greater as a corporate business leader, a scientist, a lawyer, or a politician. The world and work of the ordained minister may not seem as vital or crucial to the future of the nation, or the world, as those of persons who wield technological, financial, political, or industrial power.

Consideration of this question requires that we start by thinking about the nature and purpose of the church, because ordained ministry cannot be separated from the church. Like Jesus Christ, the church is both human and divine. Called into being by God, the church is not just another human community, a "holy Rotary Club," to borrow a phrase from one of Flannery O'Connor's stories. It is a God-given reality, grounded in Jesus Christ, and sustained by the Holy Spirit. But, at the same time, the church is a community of human beings, and has all of the problems and possibilities of any human community.

That the church is both human and divine is sometimes forgotten, or not even understood by Christians. This dual reality gives us perspective. When we get frustrated or discouraged with the church, we remember that what we see and experience at any given time is not the whole story. The whole story goes back to the earliest Christian community, to the Resurrection of Jesus, and to Pentecost; and it goes forward to the fulfillment of God's kingdom, which will come in God's own time. We need ever to keep before us the vision of the greatness of the church, as it has gone before us, and as it will come after us. Our role is to seek to be worthy of the Christian heritage, and to leave a proper inheritance for our successors.

In Western culture, the church was at one time the dominant institution. From the beginning of the United States, the Christian churches, and especially the mainline Protestant churches, were major shapers of the culture, wielding enormous influence. The ordained ministry was viewed as an important and powerful vocation to which some of the "brightest and best" young people aspired, usually with enthusiastic support from their parents. Most of the older private colleges and universities in the United States were founded by church leadership, as church institutions, to train clergy. Some sociologists and historians are now suggesting that the new pluralism of Western culture, and American culture in particular, has displaced the dominant role of the churches, and, in turn, the ministry of the churches. There has been a great deal of commentary lately about the church having moved from the center to the sidelines of society.

In fact, the churches remain strong and vital, if one looks at the life and work of actual congregations, rather than just at national institutional indicators. The Christian churches have a significant role and great influence in the United States. Furthermore, the church, because it is sacramental and mystical, cannot be understood by social scientific analysis alone. A full understanding requires the vision of faith. We must recognize the church as God's gift, as the body of Christ in the world, and as the eternal community of God's people. We live with limited perspective if we look only to statistical data and contemporary information. The Christian vision of the church takes the long view. The church is of God, and it will endure to the end of time.

When we do not maintain this vision, we are pathetically shortsighted, and contribute to our own problems. C. S. Lewis makes this point in the *Screwtape Letters,* when he has Screwtape remark to Wormwood: "One of our great allies at present is the Church itself. Do not misunderstand me. I do not mean the Church as we see her spread out through all time and space and rooted in eternity, terrible as an army with banners. That I confess is a spectacle which makes our boldest tempters uneasy. But fortunately it is quite invisible to these humans."

This vision allows us to see that service in the ministry of the church is not just work for a human institution, but work for a God-given community of eternal significance. We must be informed by this vision when we consider the call to the ordained ministry of the church. The ministry of the church is about service which lifts the energies, imaginations, and spirits of men and women to God. It is in God that we come to our true identity and purpose; and so, while the church is about our daily lives here and now, it is also about those things that transcend daily existence, and have to do with ultimate reality. For this reason, service in and through the church is the most important service persons can render. Christian service has to do with human pain and suffering, joy and triumph, and with the deep spiritual hunger and ultimate destiny of us all. This perspective allows us to turn our efforts and energies to the needs of human beings, and the world, with sustained vigor and commitment. The meaning of Christian discipleship is self-giving service; and despite all contrary evidence, we do not get discouraged, because we know that God's truth will prevail. "Therefore, since it is by God's mercy that we are engaged in this ministry, we do not lose heart" (2 Cor. 4:1).

When we considered objections on the part of family members, we recognized that there is no way to argue the case for the ministry in terms of worldly power, influence, or money. Yet some clergy do exercise enormous power in the ways of the world; but this is neither the norm, nor is it the authentic model of ministry that the gospel of Jesus Christ requires. It is a false model; and there should be no temptation to argue for ordained ministry in these terms. If the apparent attractions of money, power, and things are irresistible, then one should not look to ordained ministry. The truth is that worldly goods and authority are short-lived. The real question to think about, therefore, is the meaning of a "powerful profession." It may be that, in the eyes of the world, ordained ministry is not perceived as a powerful profession; but the problem is with the definition itself. Power is relative; and, therefore, the question is, "Power to what end?" There is no more powerful role than that of the clergy when it comes to the potential to exert influence for good. The ordained minister deals daily with individual lives, with the communal life of the church, and with the social life of the larger community in which the church lives. A caring, attentive, and empathetic minister can literally change the lives of individual children, young people, and adults. The same transforming role can be played for the community. Pastoral care is both individual and communal. It extends beyond times of great need to times of normal living in such a way that new possibilities are seen and grasped.

A pastor went to a parole hearing for the son of a couple in his church. The young man was in jail for passing a series of bad checks. At the hearing the parole board chair asked the pastor, "Do you think this young man will do this again?"

The pastor did not know what to say. He was not sure that he could answer with a firm "no," or even that it was his place to make such an assertion; so he turned to the prisoner and said, "Will you do it again?" Immediately the answer came, "No, pastor." Following the hearing, after the young man was released, the pastor continued to relate to the family. Just his presence was a reminder of the promise given as a result of his caring attention. The personal power of the pastoral presence helped that young man turn his life around.

The ordained minister is almost unique in our society. Not confined to an office or work place, not limited to a restricted area of concern, the minister is an ambassador of Christ and Christ's church "without portfolio." The pastor has easy and normal access to the homes, businesses, schools, hospitals, courts, prisons, community organizations, and social settings of persons from all walks and conditions of life. This reality of access offers the ordained minister a special opportunity to work with persons of differing racial, gender, and class experiences to bring about justice, healing, and reconciliation.

The model the ordained minister seeks to follow is Jesus Christ himself. That model is of one who renounced what appeared to be power in the eyes of the world, and chose instead to be obedient unto the cross. This is the model of servant identity that characterizes authentic Christian ministry. What seems to be powerful is, in the end, weakness; while what appears to be weakness is the greatest power of all. "Where is the one who is wise? Where is the scribe? Where is the debater of this age? Has not God made foolish the wisdom of the world? For since, in the wisdom of God, the world did not know God through wisdom, God decided, through the foolishness of our proclamation, to save those who believe. . . . For God's foolishness is wiser than human wisdom, and God's weakness is stronger than human strength" (1 Cor. 1:20-21, 25).

There is no easy answer to the question "How do I know if I'm called?" The answer is multifaceted and differs for each person. The questions set forth above go with the various dimensions of the call to ordained ministry. These suggestive considerations demonstrate the range of possible ways of thinking about ordained ministry. God and the church are looking for a wide range of persons, and there is no one way to receive or answer the call. If you are intrigued with the potential of ordained ministry, and if you are open to its marvelous demands and great expectations, then, by God's grace, you may grow to the conviction of call, and receive the power to respond affirmatively, "Here I am, send me!"

# 3

# The Nature of Ordained Ministry: "What Does It Mean to Be Ordained?"

*Then after fasting and praying they laid their hands on them and sent them off.*

—Acts 13:3

### God's Act in the Church

Ordination is present in every major tradition of Christianity. Even so most Christians, and many ordained ministers, cannot answer the question, "What does it mean to be ordained?" It is a question that burns in every person thinking about the professional ministry. Certain related questions also consistently arise. These include: "Why is ordination necessary?" "What does ordination allow one to do?" "What is the relation of ordination to preaching?" "What is its relation to the sacraments?" "What does ordination do to the one ordained?" All of these are important questions and point to various dimensions of the reality of ordination. In this chapter we explore these basic issues, and consider several other aspects of ordination for the person contemplating the invitation to the church's ordained ministry.

When making "an invitation to the *church's* ordained ministry," we emphasize that this ministry does not belong to any individual, but is fundamentally a communal reality. It is not unusual to hear pastors talk about "my ministry." "I began my ministry in 1968." "In the course of my ministry I have had three churches." To be fair, this is not usually intended to be a selfish expression, but rather a reference to a "career"; but I urge you to avoid it. It gives the wrong impression, and subtly perpetuates the idea that ministry belongs to the ordained. Ordination belongs to the *church* and is never rightly thought of as a "credential" possessed by an individual, allowing that individual to "practice" ministry. When we say that ordination belongs to the church, we must remember that the church is the community of God's people. As a God-given reality, the church transcends its existence as a human community; but, as a human community, it must have leadership. The church is given leadership by God so that it can function in the world.

The leadership God gives the church takes many different forms and involves a wide variety of people, as we saw in the first chapter on Christian vocation. One form of leadership is that of ordained ministry, a gift from God to the church, and an act of God in the church. Putting it this way points to the fact that ordination is not just a human reality, in which the church, as a human community, establishes leadership; but it is God's reality, in which the Holy Spirit empowers leadership for the sake of the Christian community. Both the Old and New Testaments demonstrate that the Lord has always raised up leadership for the people of God.

*1. Leadership in the Old Testament.* The book of Numbers states that God gives leadership so "that the congregation of the Lord may not be as sheep without a shepherd" (Num.

27:17). In Leviticus 24 laws concerning priestly leadership for the people are given, and a distinction is noted concerning those set aside as "priests," for leadership in worship, and the others of the community; this would later be similar to the distinction made between "clergy" and "laity." The story of Joshua, in Deuteronomy 34, represents leadership for preservation and governance. It is clear that he was "commissioned" according to the direction of the Lord; and this "commissioning" was symbolized by the fact that Moses "laid his hands upon him" (Deut. 34:9). In the last chapter we considered the prophetic leadership called forth by God in Isaiah 6; another example is that of Jeremiah: "Before I formed you in the womb I knew you, and before you were born I consecrated you; I appointed you a prophet to the nations" (Jer. 1:5). Ezra is entrusted with the leadership of teaching and interpreting the Scriptures, and informing the people of their traditions: "For Ezra had set his heart to study the law of the Lord, and to do it, and to teach the statutes and ordinances in Israel" (Ezra 7:10). As these examples demonstrate, leadership in the Old Testament was for a number of purposes: *preservation and governance of the community, worship leadership, prophetic proclamation, and teaching of the Scriptures and the traditions of Israel.* These same purposes characterize the leadership God later provided for Christianity, the new Israel.

*2. Leadership in the early church.* In the earliest church, as evidenced in the letters of Paul, leadership was recognized as a gift of the Spirit, and was largely informal, diverse, and functional: "And his gifts were that some should be apostles, some prophets, some evangelists, some pastors and teachers, for the equipment of the saints, for the work of ministry, for building up the body of Christ" (Eph. 4:11-12). Within the New Testament, however, we also see gradual specification of functions. By the time of the later New Testament writings, there is clear delineation of "offices" of ministry. For instance, in 1 Timothy 3, we get what amount to job descriptions for a bishop (*episkopos*) and for a deacon (*diakonos*); and in Titus 1:5-9 there is a job description for the office of elder, or presbyter (*presbyteros*). This provision of organization for leadership, under the guidance of the Holy Spirit, can be understood as a gradual institutionalization of the church, so that it could function as a community in the world.

The early Christian community grew out of Judaism. Jesus and his followers were Jews. It is only natural that, in the years after Jesus' resurrection, the followers of Christ would look to their Jewish heritage to understand, to find models for, and to develop patterns for authorizing, the leadership God was providing for them. In the Old Testament leaders were designated through the laying on of hands with prayer. The laying on of hands was an authorizing of leadership by one generation for another. The hands passed on responsibility and accountability. Those who had hands laid upon them were commissioned to lead in accordance with the tradition; and to lead into the future, with the guidance of God's spirit, whose presence was invoked with prayer. Those chosen were intended to be worthy of the trust of the people; and they were expected to act not out of their own interest or inclination, but out of the interest of the community, in accord with God's spirit. The same intention informed the shaping of leadership for the early church. Christianity absorbed images and actions from the Jewish community to recognize and confer authority on its leaders. Leadership was a sacred commission passed on by designated leaders in an effort to assure trustworthiness. In a way similar to that in the Old Testament, leadership was set apart through prayer and the laying on of hands.

3. *Offices and orders of leadership.* The church also inherited patterns of Jewish leadership. An example is the office of

elder (or presbyter). In Israel, the council of elders was an official group of revered leaders who were set aside to play a special role in teaching, advising, and ordering the community. Ordained rabbis stand in this tradition in modern Judaism. The Christian office of presbyter (*presbyteros*) came from this Jewish pattern of a council (or college) of elders. The office of presbyter is the root of the order of the priesthood in the Roman Catholic, Orthodox, and Anglican traditions, and the basis for the office of ordained minister in the Protestant churches. The invitation to consider the call to the church's ordained ministry is really an invitation to explore this office of presbyter, because it is the office in which most ordained Christian ministers serve throughout the world today.

In addition to the influence of its Jewish roots, the church drew upon the images and forms of leadership within the governmental organization of the Roman Empire, in which it lived and grew. The office of "bishop" (*episkopos*) was adapted from secular roles in the Roman Empire. The word literally means "overseer" or "superintendent," and refers to one who provides oversight for a community in a particular geographical setting. Originally the bishop served as the pastor of a church in a specific community. The bishop manifested the unity and continuity of the church, and was charged with responsibility for apostolic teaching about what the church was to believe and how the church was to live. Gradually, as the church grew, the bishop took on a supervisory role in larger geographical areas. As this happened, presbyters, as "assistants to the bishop," were given responsibility for local congregations. The church gradually merged the pattern of leadership represented by elders and that represented by bishops.

Today bishops continue to represent the apostolic continuity and unity of the church; this role is exemplified in

numerous ways, but particularly by their part in the ordination of other ministers. In the Roman Catholic, Orthodox,
and Anglican churches they characterize the fullness of the
church's ministry. In all churches which have bishops, they
serve in the role of superintending pastors, providing oversight, as they minister with other clergy and laity. Many
Protestant and Reformed churches do not have "bishops,"
although there is usually some provision for signs of apostolicity, catholicity, and unity. Most Protestant churches have
an office in which persons serve who are charged with the
oversight, or "superintending," of the larger church beyond
specific congregations, as well as representation of the shared
ministries of the church.

Another important early office is the diaconate. While the
term *diakonia* is widely used in the New Testament to refer
to the service of Jesus, and of all Christians, already in the
Book of Acts some persons are given the specific designation
"deacon." The later New Testament writings describe an
"office" of "deacon" (*diakonos*). The office was related to the
bishop, and seems to have functioned as an extension of the
work of the bishop. Eventually the diaconate became a
"stepping stone" to the presbyterate; although the presbyter
did not cease to be a deacon as well. Reevaluation and change
is on the horizon in almost all of the churches about the role
of diaconal ministry. The office is being renewed. In some
churches the renewal is taking the form of a permanent
ordained deacon. This means that some persons are ordained
as deacons for life, and some are ordained as deacons who will
later also be ordained as presbyters. There is also theological
exploration of the idea of eliminating the transitional character of the diaconate altogether, and having only the office
of permanent deacon, in which case presbyters would not
first be ordained deacons.

The New Testament writings link the bishop and deacon

together, while the office of presbyter is distinct from both; although sometimes the presbyter and bishop seem to be essentially one, both in the Scriptures (see Titus 1:5-9), and in the early church. We know that in the early church it was not necessary to be a presbyter prior to service as a bishop; this tradition developed later. No formal organization specified the exact relationship among the offices of ministry in the early church. The development of established patterns took hundreds of years; and the history of Christian ministry suggests that there is continual development of new forms and patterns. This development continues into our time in all of the churches. The church's ministry responds, through the guidance of the Holy Spirit, as the needs and conditions of both church and society change.

Although there is unclarity about the exact roles of deacon, bishop, and presbyter in both the Scriptures and the early church, these historic offices are the basis of the church's ordained ministry. The ordained ministry should be thought of as a single ministry whose oneness is characterized by the service of Word and sacrament. Together ordained ministers are the Christian "clergy." The term *clergy* (*kleros*) refers to those set apart by the community, and commissioned to know, preserve, and interpret the community's Scriptures and tradition, to administer the sacraments, lead in worship, and provide pastoral care and oversight. The church designated persons for service and appointed them to the clerical offices by the laying on of hands with prayer. This act came to be known as "ordination." The idea and reality of an ordained ministry of and for the church was a development within the earliest church. *All major traditions within Christianity set some members apart for the particular ministry of Word and sacrament. In all of the churches, there is a recognized need for persons to serve as ordained ministers.*

4. *The meaning of ordination.* The specific act of ordina-

tion takes place in various ways within Christian churches; but it always involves the laying on of hands with prayer. As we have seen, this tradition grew out of the Old Testament; and, within Christianity, it goes back to the earliest days of the church. The passage from the Book of Acts used as the text for this chapter is an example. The story tells of the setting apart of Barnabas and Saul by the church in Antioch. The community was gathered for worship, and while they were worshiping, the Holy Spirit directed them to "set apart for me Barnabas and Saul for the work to which I have called them." The report continues: "Then after fasting and praying they laid their hands on them and sent them off" (Acts 13:2-3). This is not to be thought of as "ordination" in the sense that it would later be conceived by the early church, but it illustrates that from the beginning, the church set aside leaders through prayer and the laying on of hands.

The church confirms the call of God in candidates for ministry and decides who should be its ordained leaders, but in the act of ordination itself, the principal actor is God, through the Holy Spirit. The gathered assembly invokes God's presence, and prays that the grace of the Holy Spirit will be given to empower the ministry of the one ordained for the sake of the church. The emphasis is on what God is doing for the church, through the provision of leadership for sacramental ministries, preaching and proclamation, teaching, prophetic ministries, and the ordering and governance of the community.

Ordination is a sign to God's people of legitimate and authentic ministry. It serves the church by signaling that the one ordained is recognized by the church, as represented by the ordaining authorities, as one who can be trusted to be faithful to the gospel, as expressed in the apostolic teaching, in every and all aspects of the work of the ministry. *Ordination literally creates a group of servants for the church.* Ordination empowers, commissions, and allows one to preach and teach the Word of God, to administer the sacraments to the people, and to order the life of the church. Preaching and teaching are linked to ordination because it is the faith of the church, and not simply what one individual thinks that needs to be communicated. Ordination is linked to the ordering and governing of the church because the care and preservation of God's faithful community has always been a sacred duty entrusted to those who will carry this out on behalf of the people in accord with the gospel. Ordination is linked with the sacramental ministries because it is in the sacraments that the gospel is expressed in its wholeness. In the "sign acts" of the sacraments God's grace is communicated in a unique way, through the presence of Jesus Christ and the Holy Spirit in the church. The presiding officer in the sacramental ministries must be one entrusted to abide by the historic faith, and the fullness of the teachings of the gospel, as they are made manifest in the gathered community. The ordained minister is not an individual actor, but one who is serving in an office commissioned by the church for its good. It is an office given by God, and accepted and continued by the church, to serve God's people.

What, exactly, does ordination do to the one ordained? Because of the theological emphasis on the action of God in setting leadership apart, the Roman Catholic Church, over the course of many centuries, came to teach that ordination is a sacrament. A sacrament is an outward and visible sign of an inward and invisible grace. Understanding ordination as a sacrament emphasizes the *objective* nature of what happens in the laying on of hands with prayer. The idea is that God's action not only sets one apart for leadership, but actually changes the person, and imparts a "priestly character" which will last forever. A distinction is made between the "person" and the "office." The ordained minister is still a "person," with all of the normal human possibilities and problems, but the ordained minister is also one who holds an "office" of divine origin, which transcends the inadequacies of any individual. The mystery of incarnation is signified in the uniting of a divine office with a human person. The greatness of this way of thinking about ordination is that it elevates the *office* of the ordained minister, and reminds the church that the office is given by God, for the good of the church, as a channel of God's saving grace.

Protestants, since the Reformation of the sixteenth century, have thought of ordination in more *subjective* terms. While there is not an objective change in the person ordained, the person is given authority to exercise a sacred office in and for the church. Ordination confers a role in the community for the ministries of Word and sacrament. Sometimes popular Protestant thinking has reduced ordination to a kind of credentialing. Most Protestant theology, however, has emphasized the reality of ordination as God's act, through the Holy Spirit, in the church. In this sense, ordination does alter the identity of the one who is ordained, because that person is bound to the fullness of the church and its ministry, and becomes an official representative of and to the church.

Recent work on the theology of ministry in virtually all of the churches is bringing about some ecumenical convergences in thinking about ordination. Older ways of expressing the meaning of ordination are giving way to expressions less concerned with "objectivity" or "subjectivity" and more interested in expressing what it means for God and the church to set persons aside for leadership in the Christian community. This way of thinking emphasizes the role of the ordained minister in the community of believers. Ordination has meaning in the context of the church community; and authority is manifested in a living, worshiping community of Christians, who are served by the ordained person.

Why is ordination necessary? In the early church there was concern that the Scriptures be read and taught according to the apostolic tradition, that the apostolic faith itself be taught with accuracy and care, and that the community of believers in each place not take on the shape of its particular leader, but be ordered in relationship to the larger church. As the church began to grow rapidly, there was danger that leaders might not know the Scriptures, and that they might not be acquainted with the fullness of teaching represented by the faith first given to, and passed on by, the apostles. For this reason the church developed a pattern of leadership in which those who were ordained were given responsibility for learning and teaching the Scriptures and the faith according to the "tradition." This was for the protection of the church. It was service to the people, to assure that what was taught was not just what the leaders wanted to teach, or what they thought about something, but that it might be consistent and accountable to wider Christian teaching. The ordained minister was charged to teach the received faith of the apostles, in every place, so that the church would be one. Ordination is a gift of God to help assure apostolicity, catholicity, and unity, signs of the church of Jesus Christ.

The point at which the gospel message is made most concrete is in the celebration of the Eucharist, the Holy Communion, or the Lord's Supper. Here the essential message of the gospel is set out through Scripture, through teaching, and through "sign act." The combination of these powerful responsibilities requires that for the sake of the church, there be certainty that what is taught, done, and communicated is in accord with the apostolic faith. The authenticity of the sacrament is at stake. Thus the leadership of the ordained minister at the table of the Lord is for the service of the people; it is not because the ordained minister is "above" them, or part of an "elite." At the Lord's Table, more than anywhere else, the purpose of ordained ministry is made clear. That purpose is service. The sacramental minister is the servant of the servants of God.

## Representative Character

Among the greatest privileges of ordained ministry is that one is allowed to serve as a representative figure. The representative nature of ordained ministry has several aspects. One is to represent the church to God; a second is to represent the servant role of Christ to the church; a third is to represent the servant role of the church, as the body of Christ, to the world. In the liturgical role of worship leadership in the congregation of God's people, the ordained minister serves as the "president" of the worshiping community. The gathered life of the congregation is symbolically lifted to the Lord by the representative leader. In regard to the second aspect, it should be specified that the representation of Christ to the church is not to be thought of as a literal representation, or "taking the place" of Christ. Christ is unique, and therefore the meaning of representation is that the ordained minister is the person in the congregation who brings to focus the shared servant ministry. It is not the individuality of the pastor as person, or even as friend, that matters, but the role of the pastor as the one who symbolizes the total Christian proclamation.

I remember once being called to the home of a parishioner who had died. The call came while I was talking with another member of the congregation, a physician who happened to be the son and brother of ordained ministers. As I hung up the telephone I told him that I had to leave to go to the home of the widow and children. He commented, "Remember, Dennis, they do not want you there as friend, but as their pastor." When I got to the house, the new widow met me in the front hall and ushered me into the front room where numerous members of the family and close friends had gathered. As she did so she announced, "The pastor is here." Most important in that moment was not that I was Dennis Campbell, but that I was "the pastor." Now obviously the way I made that pastoral call, my individuality, my personality, my style mattered, but what really mattered was that I was there as a representative figure. When I walked in the door, I was not there as another friend or family member, come to express grief and support; I was there as the "representative" of the Christian gospel and of the church community.

In a similar way, the ordained minister is a representative figure in relationship to the larger community. Members of the clergy bring a certain expertise to their multiple roles in the general society; but, just as importantly, in their own presence, they bring the presence of the church. Whether we like it or not, those who are not a part of the church often know Christianity chiefly through the lives and activities of the clergy. One way of thinking about the representative role of the ordained minister is to understand that ordination involves taking upon oneself an "official" position. The ordained minister holds an "office." Because we hold an office, we act not just for ourselves, or in our own name, but in the name of the community which has entrusted to us this "official" position.

In the early church one of the qualities expected of ordained leaders was that they could go to their deaths firm in their affirmation of Jesus Christ. During periods of persecution, the first Christians to be killed were the "official" leaders of the church. These official leaders were the ordained ministers who represented the Christian community to the larger society. It was important, therefore, that these persons be able to maintain the integrity of the faith in the face of severe trial and even death. Most clergy do not face this severe test of their representative character, but examples can be found. Christian missionaries worked in Uganda during the regime of Idi Amin. Amin routinely persecuted Christians. It brought the churches close together, because Amin made no distinction between Anglicans, Baptists, Roman Catholics, or Lutherans. To him, they were all the same. And he always went first for the leadership. Among the martyrs was the Anglican archbishop. In such a setting, the faithfulness of the "official" leadership of the church was a moving witness to all the world. This same kind of faithfulness characterized much of the ordained leadership of the churches in Eastern Europe during Communist persecutions.

In the summer of 1987, Eugenio Poma was elected bishop of the Methodist Church in Bolivia. Eugenio Poma is an Aymara Indian whose whole life has been given to the improvement of his people. Bishop Leontine Kelly was in Bolivia to participate in his consecration. Afterwards she went with him when he made the long journey high into the Andes to his tiny native village to tell his aged mother that he was now a bishop of the church. When he told his mother, she burst into tears, and turned to him with searching eyes saying, "Why don't you just come back and farm this land?" Bishop Kelly could not understand this mother's reaction; but later Bishop Poma told her that his mother associated the leadership of the church with martyrdom. She was afraid that he would be killed for what the church stands for in the rural Andes of Bolivia.

The representative character of ordained ministry is one of the reasons that no person has the "right" to be ordained. It is the responsibility of the church to establish expectations and qualifications, and then to determine which persons are appropriate for the representative role. The church must be satisfied that those who are ordained are willing and able to take upon themselves the requisite official and public roles. What ordained ministers say and do, the way in which they live their lives, everything about them, has significance; because they have willingly taken upon themselves the opportunity to live the Christian life in the church and in the world as official representatives of Christ and the ministries of the church.

**Collegial Character**

The ministry of the church is a corporate reality shared by all Christians. In a similar, but more specific way, ordained ministry is shared by those who are called to this particular ministry. Being ordained means that one joins a company of persons to whom one is accountable, and for whom one is accountable. The idea of a shared ministry of ordained clergy is like that of the collegial service rendered by the council of elders in the Jewish tradition. The council of elders included those to whom the community looked for general leadership, but especially for teaching. The council instructed new members, so that they learned the tradition, and could be trusted to instruct others. *College* is another word often used in the Christian tradition to refer to a council of clergy. When we use the term *college* we usually think of a school; but the original meaning of the word was a group of clergy who lived together, and who were charged with certain responsibilities. Usually they were scholars and teachers; and they often received students, which explains the reason that the term later came to be used popularly in reference to a school. A hallmark of a college of clergy is that every individual is subject to the whole, for the good of the church. This manifests the essential principle that ordained Christian ministry is a collegial reality.

If you are an ordained minister, you are a member of a

"college," a community of elders in the faith, who have been trained, and have the responsibility to serve the church, not according to individual preferences, interests, or inclinations, but according to the shared ministry of the gospel. The college does not exist for its own sake, but for the sake of the community. Ordained ministers are not "solo practitioners," nor do they exist in isolation. Their authenticity is related to the corporate character of their vocation.

There is no greater bond of relationship than that which exists among sisters and brothers who share the call to ordained ministry, and exercise that call in the churches of the Christian faith throughout the world. A friend recently told me about a comment made to him, at the time of his ordination, by an elderly pastor: "Welcome to the sweetest communion this side of heaven." My uncle Gideon Carlson was a pastor. He loved his colleagues in the Methodist connection, and had a strong sense of obligation to them. Not only seeing to it that the parsonage was clean and in order when he moved on to a new charge, but also that his preaching and teaching were faithful to the Christian tradition, so that the one who followed him would find that he had been responsible, that the parish was in order, and that it was ready gladly to welcome the next pastor. He recognized that there were varieties of gifts among his colleagues in ministry. Not all the preachers in rural Illinois were like him. And yet each had gifts; and diversity enriched the church. We are yoked in a common effort; and it is in the common effort that ministry thrives.

The sense of community among persons in shared ministry is a gift from God. Ordained ministers are not in competition with one another; their success is not dependent on outdoing one another; their interest is not served by another's failure. Though there are differences of tradition, style, and approach, the common affirmation of Jesus Christ transcends the differences, and there is recognition of authentic Christian ministry. As you consider the invitation to the church's ordained ministry, you should know that the opportunity to work together with others, who are also called and appointed to this collegial servant ministry, for the upbuilding of the kingdom of God, is one of the unique privileges of this special vocation.

## The Moral Life

What is expected of the ordained minister, in terms of the moral life, does not differ from what is expected of any Christian believer. There is not a separate standard of moral practice which sets aside one who is ordained. What is different, however, is that the ordained minister has willingly accepted the representative character of ordination. Therefore, while the expectations of the moral life are the same for all Christians, the "official" role of the clergy means that our actions and behaviors are not only our own, but they also officially represent the church. This is the chief reason why moral lapses on the part of the clergy are so serious and so regrettable. It is not that the clergy's sins are worse, in and of themselves, but they are worse because they do "official" harm to the Christian community.

Candidates for ordained ministry invariably want to know about issues having to do with human sexuality. The expectations for ordained ministers, in most of the churches, are not different from those for all Christians. The teaching of the church about the way any responsible Christian is expected to exercise the gift of sexuality given by God applies to the ordained minister. Throughout the history of Christianity, the teaching of all the major churches has been that the Bible and Christian tradition require that Christians exercise their sexuality either in the context of heterosexual monogamous marriage, or in celibacy. This is the teaching of virtually all Christian churches today. Recent studies and discussion about the nature of homosexuality have stimulated reflection, new thinking, and proposals for alternative approaches in some churches. The major point is that the churches have always expected those who are ordained to live by the same standards recommended to the whole people of God. An exception is the insistence on celibacy for its clergy on the part of the Roman Catholic Church. Celibacy has always been one of the options for the exercising of God's gift of sexuality on the part of all Christians, but in the case of the Roman Catholic Church, it is a specific standard for the clergy. The vow of celibacy is intended to free one from the obligations of spouse and family so that the mission of the church can be given undivided attention.

A person thinking about the call to ordained ministry should early come to terms with the fact that issues of human sexuality in relation to the clergy are getting a great deal of attention. Problems with promiscuity on the part of clergy are dreadfully harmful not only to the persons involved, but to the whole church. The power traditionally associated with the clerical role can offer occasion for a variety of abusive relationships with others, both adults and children. The churches must deal with these ugly truths and seek diligently to end and prevent such incidents among its clergy. Ordained ministers are not perfect, and perfection cannot be expected. But their actions reflect publicly on the church in a serious way, because they are officially representative of the church. If you accept the invitation to ordained ministry, you must understand the importance of everything you do, and commit yourself to live an exemplary life for the sake of Christ and the church.

During your time of discernment, you will probably be asked to undergo psychological testing and counseling. It is possible to raise theological objections to psychological testing for ministry. Some great Christian leaders might not have passed. Nevertheless, psychological tests are one way for the churches to learn more about candidates; and such legitimate efforts are needed if they can help prevent persons who might be prone to abusive relationships from being ordained. The results of psychological tests and counseling are one part of the total picture considered by the church prior to the ordination of a candidate.

Another area of moral urgency is that of financial responsibility. Members of the clergy have a special obligation to order their lives in such a way that they are above reproach in all financial dealings. Again, there is nothing unique in regard to financial accountability that distinguishes clergy and laity; but because of the representative character of the ordained, the obligations are particularly acute. Perhaps it should not surprise us that most of the scandals in recent years involving ordained ministers have resulted from serious abuse of sex, money, or power. The humanity and potential for sinful behavior on the part of ordained ministers are acutely evident in these areas.

At root of many mistakes made by the clergy in regard to the moral life are ego and pride. There are many ego rewards from ordained ministry, and such rewards can be a source of pride. The dangers that come with being accorded a special role are severe when they are mixed up with religion. Jesus' counsel concerning humility is therefore particularly essential for the ordained minister. Overall, the moral life is a primary means of communication of the gospel. The call to ordained ministry includes the invitation to live a life that is exemplary. Think about ministry as requiring "authenticity." The life of the ordained minister must be authentic, and in order for this to be so, all aspects of one's total life must fit together as a whole. The emphasis is on the character of the pastor, and not on individual acts. The total life of the ordained minister represents Christ and the church, and is officially a sign unto the church and unto the world.

### Placed According to God's Will

Persons who are thinking about the call to ordained ministry often worry about the matter of placement. The major church bodies have varying ways of bringing congregational needs and pastoral services together. In some, all pastors are appointed by the bishop, or a stationing committee; in some, congregations call pastors; in some, there is a combination of local and denominational authority in which lay committees in congregations work with suggestions given to them by a bishop, or representatives of a presbytery, synod, conference, or other judicatory. Usually in such cases the congregation ultimately issues the call. The Bible prescribes no one way, nor does the history of Christianity, for a pastor and people to be brought together. Neither is there a perfect system in sociological, administrative, or management theory. Nevertheless, the various traditions within Christianity have well-established processes. These processes have changed through the years, and are constantly changing, in order to deal with differing times and needs.

Good and appropriate work is always available for any ordained minister who is willing to serve the church without an unusual set of complex personal requirements. If you hear an ordained minister complaining about placement, usually it is because the expectations are that the church will accommodate particular needs or desires of a pastor. Sometimes these complexities are necessary and understandable to churches. Spousal employment, parental responsibilities, or health concerns are some examples. But no church is obliged to make special arrangements to accommodate the needs or demands of its ordained clergy. There are limits to what can or should be done. One responds to the call of God and the church not to satisfy one's own needs and desires, but to be in service.

Not all ordained ministers are pastors of congregations; but even in such cases, consideration must be given to the priority of the communal nature of the church's ministry. The ordained minister is not an independent professional out seeking a job. Ordination has meaning only in relationship to the needs of the church and its corporate life. Ordained ministry is always linked to the actual life of congregations of Christian people, where leadership of Word and sacrament is exercised regularly and faithfully.

When considering ordained ministry, always think first about the matter of placement theologically, rather than in administrative, sociological, or demographical terms. A theological perspective requires us to remember that one is called to ordained ministry by God and the church. Therefore, we should not approach placement as if we were simply in the market for a job. Our attitude about placement will largely determine the effectiveness of our ministry. Most ordained ministers will tell you that some of their best and most rewarding service has been rendered in settings they would not have imagined or chosen on their own. A hymn written by Charles Wesley, in 1740, expresses God's providential role in placement. The hymn, based on 1 Corinthians 12:4-31 and Galatians 3:27-28, is about the nature of the church as the body of Christ, and what that means for those who are its members. Every member makes an important contribution. The contribution we make is not a matter of our own preference, however; because God gives different gifts, and all are important, but not all are the same. How we exercise those gifts, and where we exercise them, will differ according to God's will. All are important to the whole:

Move and actuate and guide,
diverse gifts to each divide;
placed according to thy will,
let us all our work fulfill.

The idea that we are placed according to God's will is a profound theological insight particularly essential to thinking about ordained ministry.

Some years ago a former student, in letter after letter, articulated different options and possibilities for his future. The different options were debated, and he made an effort to assess the possibilities according to a calculus of probability. After several letters like this I became weary of the obvious self-interested ambition. I commented in a letter to him that a "calculated" ministry not only would not bring happiness, it was certain to bring frustration and despair because it would result in spiritual bankruptcy. If one's primary concern is to answer the call of God and the church in order to be in service, then placement will not be a problem. It is only when one wants to use the church to meet one's own needs, desires, and ambitions that problems arise.

I do not mean that no personal considerations can or should enter into the matter of where and how ordained ministry is exercised. Many opportunities will allow you to express preferences, to influence directions, and even to make specific choices. The issue is *priority*. If the *priority* is meeting one's own wants, then there is something wrong; because ordained ministry is not, in the first place, about meeting one's own wants. There are other ways to do that. The greatness of the ordained ministry is that life is dedicated, *in the first place,* to service. The amazing thing is that if one's priorities are right, more often than not, genuine satisfaction follows in unanticipated and delightful ways. Usually we do not even know what to desire. If we give them time, God's surprises produce unexpected joys.

## Rewards

What about the rewards of the church's professional ordained ministry? The question of financial compensation inevitably arises. You should think about this in a way that is consistent with all of our other considerations of the ministry. In the first place, one is not in ordained ministry to "make a living." This essential conceptual understanding must come before all else. Ordained ministers are not "paid for their work." The Christian community gets together and provides sufficient support to make it possible for one to serve full time in the leadership of the church. If it is put in these terms, we think about financial compensation as "honorarium," rather than as "pay," or even as "salary."

Once in a while you might confess to feeling that it is "unfair" that ordained ministry requires a graduate professional degree, just like law or medicine, but the churches do not feel that it is incumbent on them to pay a "salary" comparable to "other professionals." This way of thinking is based on a wrong model of ministry; and it will lead to frustration and unhappiness. Ordained ministers are representative figures, and the way they live is itself a sign to the church and the world. The churches provide sufficient support, generally including housing and other benefits, to allow the pastor to live appropriately. No one need hesitate to respond with enthusiasm to the call to ordained ministry for fear of not having sufficient resources. The key is to think about what is really important, and to understand that financial compensation is only one of the multiple rewards of professional ministry.

In fact it is almost embarrassing that the ordained ministry provides such abundant rewards beyond basic support for satisfactory living. One of the most significant is the opportunity to be set free to be in ministry. No one tells the ordained minister what to do every day. You are in control of your own schedule, and have the opportunity to establish priorities. It is the job of the ordained minister to know what needs to be done, and what is most important. The pastor also has the privilege of work that is perpetually diverse and endlessly interesting. Hardly any day will be the same as the day before, because people's needs are variable, and the demands are always changing. The role played by the pastor in the congregation, and in the larger community outside of the church, is sufficiently flexible as to accommodate special emphases. This means that the unique interests, abilities, and skills of the ordained minister can and will be used. We are not each alike, nor do we behave the same way.

There is immense satisfaction in having the chance to make a difference in individual lives, as well as in the lives of families, groups, and even whole communities. Pastors are able to see results of their work with people; and the appreciation voiced, even years later, is compensation indeed. But the greatest reward of the ordained ministry is the knowledge that one's life is being invested in an enterprise that is, in the end, not transient but permanent and eternal. The conviction that you are giving yourself to a greater, transcendent good is a reward worth more than any money in the world.

# CHAPTER 4

# The Work of the Ordained Ministry: "What Are the Things I Would Do?"

*Tend the flock of God that is in your charge, exercising the oversight, not under compulsion but willingly, as God would have you do it—not for sordid gain but eagerly. Do not lord it over those in your charge, but be examples to the flock.*

—1 Peter 5:2-3

## The Pastoral Office

The ordained ministry of the church propels one into some of the most interesting work available; but many people have little notion of what it is that a pastor does all day. Consider the old joke that the pastor works only on Sunday mornings. We really know better; although the nature and range of a pastor's responsibilities are largely unknown. In this chapter you will gain an idea of the kinds of things that an ordained minister does. Not all ordained ministers are pastors of congregations. Many serve in other roles such as college, hospital, military, or prison chaplains; college or university professors; pastoral counselors; writers or publishers; or administrators of schools, colleges, seminaries, hospitals, homes, or other church-related institutions. At root, however, is a *core identity which characterizes the ordained minister.* This core identity is given and received in ordination, and includes the multiple factors we considered in the last chapter. The core identity manifests itself in the role of pastor. In whatever setting an ordained minister serves, it is the *pastoral office* that characterizes and defines the service.

The ordained minister is commissioned to "tend the flock of God that is your charge" (1 Pet. 5:2). Shepherd imagery for pastoral ministry is fundamental to the whole Bible. Old Testament writers pictured the promised one of Israel as a shepherd: "He will feed his flock like a shepherd, he will gather the lambs in his arms" (Isa. 40:11). The church understands Jesus Christ as the "great shepherd of the sheep" (Heb. 13:20). Jesus is himself the chief shepherd; and the church applies this shepherd image to its pastors. That is the origin of the word *pastor.*

As we saw in the last chapter, there are many terms, or titles, used for ordained ministers. This is because the ministry has many aspects, and the various titles used tend to emphasize one or another aspect of the total work. The pastoral office and role encompasses them all, however, and is characteristic of all Christian traditions. No matter what it is that the ordained minister is doing, the pastoral identity is and must be apparent. This identity is inherent regardless of the specific job performed or the context in which the pastor serves. In this chapter we will look at what it is that a pastor does. Most references will be to service in a congregation, but we are looking at the nature and identity of the pastor, no matter where pastoral service is rendered. All of the various roles involved in the work of the ordained minister apply, in some way, in every setting, because they are constitutive of fundamental pastoral identity, not of any particular job or place of service.

### Is Ordained Ministry a Profession?

Churches often use the term "professional ministry" to refer to the clergy. The intention is to indicate the difference between the ministry of the whole people of God and that of those who are set aside for full-time service as pastors. Much debate and discussion throughout the twentieth century attended the use of the term *professional* in regard to ordained ministry. Many persons in the church object to such language because it seems to suggest that ordained ministry is just another job among jobs. This, they think, leads to "careerism," in which the full-time ministry of the church is treated as a "job" rather than a "calling." Perhaps the greatest difficulty with the whole discussion is the lack of clarity about the meaning of "profession."

The term *profession* grew out of the medieval Christian church. It was used by orders of monks and nuns in reference to their profession of Christianity and, more specifically, to their profession of religious vows. Persons in these religious orders took upon themselves responsibility for a number of necessary social services for the whole community. Few people were educated, and most of them were religious "professionals." These religious professionals served the society in the early developments of the fields of medicine and law, as well as in their primary commitment to theology. What propelled them into these fields was their first commitment to serve the real needs of people in society. Gradually they created fields of expertise which were taught in the early universities. Religious communities founded universities to be of service. This service included not only advancement of the traditional learning of Western culture but also education in the specialized knowledge required for the professions.

The three classic professions are divinity, medicine, and law. Each of them has a long intellectual tradition; and the classic definition of a university includes the expectation that it have faculties in each of these fields. In their early period, the universities of Western Europe were clerical foundations; and the faculties were, first of all, religious professionals. Most of the faculty, in all fields, were ordained ministers.

A classic definition of a profession therefore grows out of this rootage in the ordained ministry of the church. There are eight defining characteristics of a profession:

1. A profession provides a social service that is essential and unique.

2. A profession involves a high degree of knowledge.

3. A profession requires of its members the ability to apply the special body of knowledge to real needs in the world.

4. A profession is a group of persons (a council or college) which is autonomous and claims the right to regulate itself.

5. A profession is characterized by a code of ethics, or a set of ethical principles, which suggests that ethical concern is fundamental.

6. A profession requires of its members self-discipline; a member of a profession accepts self-discipline and personal responsibility for actions.

7. A profession is concerned not just for itself, or its own members, but for the larger society, the community.

8. A profession is committed to rendering services to persons more than to reaping financial rewards. Professionals do not work for pay but are paid so that they can work.

You will note immediately that this classic definition of a

profession bears little resemblance to the way in which the word is used popularly today. Now a great deal of cynicism is applied toward the professions because people think that they are self-serving and protectionist. Also, the characteristics of the classic profession hardly apply even to the traditional professions. Most lawyers are not self-employed professionals; a majority work for the government, or large corporations. Even doctors are increasingly employed by corporations called "health service providers"; or, if they are in private practice, are limited by government and insurance regulations in the way they practice. The emphasis on unselfish service, in which remuneration is not the first concern, is not always evident, even in the classic professions. The term *profession* is used popularly to refer to many different careers or jobs. Engineering, journalism, business, forestry, and management are examples.

When Christians reject the idea of the ordained ministry as a profession, it is because they are thinking of this recent popular use of the word to refer to careers or jobs. If that is the only meaning, then we can surely let the whole idea go. But if you will go back and look at the eight points above, you will see that, in the classic sense, ordained ministry is indeed a profession. This is so because a profession is, first and foremost, defined in regard to service. Everything else derives from this fundamental idea and commitment. What motivates the professional person in the first place is the good of the individuals and communities served rather than money, prestige, power, or material acquisitions.

It can be argued that the ordained ministry is the last best example of a classic profession in Western society. The call to ordained ministry is a call to enter a profession in which you are responsible for the eight points which characterize a profession. This high calling is not a job or career, although it may involve both of these; rather it is a profession, which calls forth a level of expectation far beyond that of making a living, or of self-fulfillment. Referring to the ordained minister as a professional involves the recognition that there is a *pastoral character and identity* which transcends any specific work, and involves a person's total life, not just one's "occupation."

The ordained minister can be thought of as the last general practitioner in Western culture. In the other professions specialization has become a dominant pattern. Increased specialization in law and medicine means that a client or patient is seldom seen "whole." It is rare that the lawyer or doctor provides care for a whole family, or sees the client or patient in terms of the total picture, including human relationships, jobs, social roles, community involvements, and other aspects of life. The pastor is not concerned exclusively with individuals, or with one aspect of life, because Christian faith moves us to community and wholeness. Christian relationships involve every area of individual and corporate existence. The pastor is necessarily concerned with all aspects of human life. Those who are served must be seen as whole persons, with all of the complex relationships, problems, needs, demands, joys, illnesses, and opportunities that attend our existence. For this reason we preserve the idea of ordained ministry as a profession. The service a professional person renders brings knowledge and skill together in a morally responsible manner for the good of individuals in their total life, and for the good of the communities in which they live.

### Jesus Christ as the Model of Service

Jesus Christ is the model for all ministry of the whole people of God, both lay and ordained. The primary nature of Christian ministry is service (*diakonia*). Jesus was among us as one who served; he "came not to be served but to serve, and to give his life as a ransom for many" (Mark 10:45). The ministry of those who are ordained is modeled in a particular way on the ministry of Christ. Jesus alone is the "great shepherd of the sheep"; but the pastoral role filled by or- dained ministers is representative of Christ to the church, and of the church to the world.

Sometimes Christians think that the role of representing Christ to the church means that the clergy provides "Christ figures" for the church. This can lead to arguments that only men should be ordained, because only men can literally represent Christ, since he was male. An Episcopal priest remarked that it helped him to communicate the problem with this argument to his parishioners by suggesting that if a woman cannot represent Christ at the altar, then by analogy, he could not represent her on the cross. Theologically there is no basis to suggest that "representing Christ to the church" means that one literally "stands in" for Christ in the pastoral acts. Instead it means that, in all of the specifically pastoral acts which constitute leadership in the church, the ordained minister is the servant of Christ, and of the congregation, in communicating and channeling God's grace to individuals, and to the gathered community. Christ alone is the high priest for his people, and chief shepherd of the flock.

Throughout its history, Christianity has looked to Christ's ministry to find its model for ordained ministry. In its reflection on the mystery and majesty of Jesus Christ, the church identified at least three roles, the historic offices of *prophet, priest,* and *king.* These roles are part of the pastoral office carried out by any ordained minister in the ministries of Word, sacrament, and order. It should be noted that this historic description of the offices of Christ is not without problems. Perhaps it is too "neat" in its division of the tasks of ministry into Word, sacrament, and order. Moreover, no typology is absolute. To celebrate Holy Communion in a church riven by conflict, thus requiring parties to be reconciled before sharing the sacrament, is prophetic; so is ordering the church in its stewardship to stress mission instead of maintenance. Nevertheless, one who is considering ordained ministry should know about these historic offices and understand that what the church has found important in them is that they all relate to important aspects of the work of Christ. It is from Christ that we are to take our cues about ministry.

The *prophetic* role involves the ministry of the Word. It includes preaching and teaching the Word of God as expressed in the Scriptures of the Old and New Testaments, and as interpreted by the church, throughout history, and in the contemporary period. Preaching and teaching are fundamental to the work of ordained ministry. One model for this came from the Old Testament council of elders. Teaching authority is given in ordination, and assumes the knowledge of the Scriptures and Christian tradition. The prophetic role involves challenging the church to live faithfully in the world in accord with the gospel. It may require bringing words of judgment, but it also involves bringing words of healing and support. These can be just as prophetic in a world prone to harsh judgments and quick criticism. There is no more prophetic message in the world today than that of the gospel. Breaking through the easy assumptions of human self-satisfaction, greed, and pride, the gospel message brings radical insight and hope.

In the *priestly role* the ordained minister embodies Christ's ministry of connection between God and humanity. By becoming human in Jesus, God accepted all of our human frailty, and so freed us from unending guilt, separation, and death. We receive God's gifts, chiefly the gift of Christ through the Holy Spirit, and give to God our thanks and praise in total life. Responding through faith to God's gift, we seek to live in the light of Christ. The church, in turn, becomes a priestly people, as a community of God's people in the world. "But you are a chosen race, a royal priesthood, a holy nation, God's own people, in order that you may proclaim the mighty acts of him who called you out of darkness into his marvelous light" (1 Pet. 2:9). This reality is embodied in the sacramental life of the church, in which the truth and reality of the gospel are expressed in their fullness. Through leadership in God's sacramental ministries, the ordained minister exemplifies the priestly role of Christ and the priestly role of the church.

Throughout its history the church has recognized and celebrated the *kingly* role of Christ. One Sunday in the Christian year is designated as "Christ the King." The kingly role of Christ refers to the fact that the world is God's creation, and that everything in it is ultimately under the dominion of Jesus Christ. This role also reminds us that the church is of God, and is intended to be shaped and governed by God's intentions. In the same way that the ordained minister is representative of Christ, without being literally "in the place of Christ," the ordained minister fulfills this role, but is never to be thought of as "king." The name has symbolic and historic significance; but, to avoid the male character of "king," it may be preferable to call this the "royal" role of Christ. The royal role does not mean that the ordained minister is superior to other Christians, or that the pastor is singularly authoritative. The Scriptures make this clear: "Do not lord it over those in your charge" (1 Pet. 5:3). The pastoral role seeks nothing for itself; rather the emphasis must always be on the unique person and work of Christ. The pastor points to the one who humbled himself, and ultimately gave his life, that we might live. In doing this, the pastor works with the congregation to help it order its life in relationship to God's intentions expressed in the gospel, and in accord with the larger church. The royal role of the ordained minister is about the sovereignty of God. It reminds us that God's order is breaking in upon the world even now, and ultimately, God's truth will prevail.

The only model of ministry that finally exhibits an abiding authenticity is that which takes seriously, and seeks to follow, the servanthood of Jesus Christ represented in the prophetic, priestly, and royal roles. In these the Christian community recognized the essential qualities which characterize ministry in the name of Christ; and it received them as gifts from God to the church.

## The Work of the Pastor

The work a pastor does has multiple aspects which grow directly out of the model of ministry which finds its identity and character in the prophetic, priestly, and royal roles of Jesus Christ. Let us examine the work of the pastor by looking at ten pastoral functions involved in ordination to Word, sacrament, and order. Although the list is numbered, the numbers are not meant to indicate an order of priority. In fact, these roles are often so interrelated as to be inseparable; and others might well put the list together in a different way.

*1. The pastor as a person of prayer and spiritual depth.* Recently a group was struggling with what is essential to include in the curriculum of a theological school. One member observed that she could not imagine why anyone would agree to take ordination vows if the life of prayer were not understood as central. One of the dangers of ordained ministry is that prayer and Bible reading can be reduced to a part of the professional expectations of the role. If this happens, Bible reading is done with a specific purpose in mind, and prayer, even if the pastor prays frequently during the day in settings of pastoral care or official meetings, can become less vital.

The development of spiritual disciplines is something that all Christians should learn. The pastor must learn these and be able to teach them. A major part of the years of education for professional ministry includes formation in spiritual development. There is no one way in which this is done, and exactly how it fits into a school's curriculum is debatable because it is much more than an academic exercise. But community worship, intentional groups of spiritual nurture, and individual time for growth with God is a crucial part of preparation for ordination. Prayer is the root of all effective ministry, and is the only possible way that a pastor can deal with the extraordinary demands that constantly arise in an unplanned way. The busyness of the pastor's day necessitates the development of a disciplined time and place for Bible reading and prayer. As with physical exercise, it is sometimes easy to put this off due to other demands. Parishioners know if the pastor is a person of spiritual depth; and one of the examples the pastor sets is that of faithful attention to this aspect of life. Devotional Bible reading is unrelated to preparation for specific sermons or teaching because one approaches the Bible in different ways for different purposes. Every effective pastor finds that an ordered program of daily Bible reading is useful in receiving God's Word for one's own spiritual growth apart from the press to teach and interpret for others.

During a time of discernment about the call of God and the church to ordained ministry, disciplined prayer is particularly important. Quiet assessment of your motivations and abilities, coupled with listening for God through Scripture and community, can liven your perception of the authenticity of call.

2. *The pastor as preacher.* The preaching role is one of the

ways ordination to Word is fulfilled; so if you accept the invitation to the ordained ministry of the church, you will be a preacher. The service of ordination includes the specific commission to "preach the Word." From the earliest period of the church's life, Christian leadership has been called to preach: "Preach the Word, be urgent in season and out of season" (2 Tim. 4:2). "Be urgent in season and out of season" is a marvelous admonition reminding us of the responsibility that accompanies this aspect of ordination. Week in and week out the pastor mounts the pulpit with a sense of urgency to preach the most wonderful and important news that has ever been given to humankind. This takes enormous discipline and work; but it is also one of the greatest opportunities for ministry because God works through preaching, and the message is the difference between life and death.

I find that persons thinking about ministry are often intimidated by the preaching role. "What will I preach about?" "I am afraid to stand in front of people." "I have a hard time speaking so that people can hear me." All of these concerns, and others, are raised. There is a continuing debate about whether preachers are "born" or "made." Some persons seem naturally gifted at communication, and able to inspire groups with effectiveness and apparent ease. Others struggle with real liabilities. Having watched countless numbers of theological students come to grips with the task of preaching, and having heard thousands of sermons, it seems to me that a prospective candidate for ordination should know several things.

First, *the message of the gospel of Jesus Christ is urgent and compelling.* This fact means that the job of the preacher is not to come up with something to preach about but to work always at proclamation of the message we have from God. This does not make the work of preaching less demanding; but it does demonstrate the significant difference between preaching and other forms of public speaking. Our purpose in preaching is not selling ourselves, or anything else of human origin; it is the effective communication of the gospel: "For what we preach is not ourselves but Jesus Christ as Lord, with ourselves as your servants for Jesus' sake" (2 Cor. 4:5).

Second, *the call to preach is a part of the call from God and the church to the ordained ministry.* The opportunity to proclaim God's Word is a great gift that merits development. The singular desire to be a faithful steward of the Christian message takes away anxiety because our pressing concern is to offer Christ. It was this inner compulsion that resulted in the Apostle Paul's statement that preaching was something he could not avoid. The good news of Jesus Christ was so life-changing that he was convinced of the necessity of sharing it with others. "For if I preach the gospel, that gives me no ground for boasting. For necessity is laid upon me. Woe to me if I do not preach the gospel!" (1 Cor. 9:16).

Third, while some persons have a natural gift for preaching, *preaching is a skill that is learned; and most persons can learn to be good preachers.* You are never fully formed as a preacher, and throughout life disciplined exercises can make you better. The key is the desire to be better, not for your own sake but for the sake of the gospel, and the people who need to hear it. It is the privilege and obligation of the ordained minister to stand in the pulpit and proclaim the gospel. This means constant thought about how the biblical message of the Christian faith can be interpreted to meet the needs of the congregation.

You must do everything possible to learn about public speaking. Preaching is different from public speaking, but it involves many of the same skills. It will do no good to have burning faith, clear theology, and original ideas if you cannot communicate effectively. One way to do this is to learn by watching and listening to other preachers. I do not mean to copy them, but to observe the variety of ways preaching is done. Another is to seek careful critique from trusted listeners, and not be defensive about what they say. The call to ordained ministry involves the commitment to become the best preacher you can be.

A fourth consideration for the person considering the preaching ministry is that *preaching is not an entertaining performance on the part of the preacher, but an event which does not finally depend on the preacher, nor the congregation, but on the grace of God, through the presence and work of the Holy Spirit.* I remember very well a sermon with which I was not happy. It seemed as though it had not come together. The development was disjointed, and I did not think it had impact because the response was polite but unenthusiastic. During the following week a young woman came to see me. She reported that as she heard the sermon her life suddenly took on new meaning, and she came to peace about a serious conflict she was having with her husband. We began a series of pastoral visits in the home, and a significant relationship developed with the couple. In the preaching event God brought change and healing; but it was not what I had done. Most preachers have had this kind of experience. I hope that my preparation and commitment helped to allow the Holy Spirit to work; but that incident reminds me that preaching is one of the mysterious ways God works in individuals and in communities.

*3. The pastor as sacramental minister.* The ordained minister is responsible for administering the sacraments to the people. Ministering in this way expresses the priestly role of Christ as God's grace is given to, and received by, faithful Christians according to the ordinances of the church. Lay persons occasionally preach, lead worship, and serve as theologians; and they regularly teach in the church. Service in the priestly role, as president of the worshiping congregation for sacramental celebrations, is reserved in every major Christian tradition for those who are ordained.

In the Roman Catholic, Orthodox, and Anglican traditions the priest's role in the sacramental ministries is recognized, even if it is not always understood. Sometimes Protestant pastors will be asked why a lay person cannot serve Holy Communion. I remember getting into a long discussion about this with an enthusiastic lay volunteer youth worker. He wanted the youth group retreat to end with Holy Communion, even though an ordained minister could not be present. He argued that Communion was a particularly meaningful worship experience with which to conclude an extended time together. On this we agreed. He continued by suggesting that he lead "an informal" service of the Lord's Supper. I explained that church teaching and practice would not permit that because of the unique character of sacramental celebrations. The sacraments are celebrated by the gathered community, according to the teachings of the church. From its early days, the church recognized that, for its own protection and preservation, it needed to assign responsibility for fidelity to certain designated members. Celebrations are under the leadership of one who has been duly authorized, and has taken life-long vows to care for the community, in a disciplined manner, conforming to the catholic and apostolic faith.

Sacramental celebrations are not to be taken lightly. They impart the grace of God to faithful Christians through words, actions, and mediating elements. In the sacraments Christ's presence is uniquely real and immediate to the believing community. New life is given through the work of the Holy Spirit. The sacraments are bound inseparably to the life, work, and ministry of Jesus Christ; and are much more than reminders of Christ's saving acts. The presence and action of God in Jesus Christ, through the Holy Spirit, are graphically real in the sacraments of the church. The sacraments are not magical. They depend on the faith of the believing church, in its historical tradition and contemporary shape. Their authenticity and power is grounded in apostolic teaching and catholic faith. For the sake of the community and its integrity, those who administer the sacraments are certified by the church as persons who know, and can be trusted to stand within, the tradition. For these reasons, the church, as the whole people of God, designates some of its number to be its sacramental servants.

*4. The pastor as worship leader.* In addition to preaching and celebrating the sacraments, if you are a pastor, you will serve in worship by presiding, reading scripture, and leading prayer. These things are sometimes done by lay persons, but the pastor is held accountable for shaping the service, and for the total worship experience. Learning the elements of a service, and how to lead God's people in a fitting manner, is required of all pastors. Worship leadership involves significant work, and is central to total pastoral effectiveness. Common worship on Sunday is the single most important time of the whole week for the Christian community. You will discover that no time or effort should be spared in making sure that everything has been done to assure its excellence.

There are also a variety of occasional services which specifically involve pastoral leadership. Perhaps the most obvious and important of these are weddings and funerals. These services place the pastor in an intimate relationship with people. Pastoral leadership in Christian marriage includes far more than the service itself. There are counseling sessions, planning meetings, the rehearsal, and social occasions. An experienced pastor knows that much more is at stake here than meets the eye. One must see beneath the superficial social aspects to the profound realities under the surface.

Much more time is required than most people realize. Similarly with funerals, you can expect private sessions with the bereaved, arrangements to be made with the church community, a service to plan, and many sessions of pastoral care long after the death.

Weddings and funerals are the occasion for extraordinary pastoral service. These central times of the human life cycle demand sensitivity and care. They bring out the best and worst in individuals and families. Often complex personal relationships among family and friends become part of the process. Tensions resulting from divorce, estrangement, or conflict, combined with the desire in almost everyone for propriety, result in exquisite dilemmas. The pastor is sought to provide a calming influence, and guidance about how to "do things right." Every pastor has a stock of favorite funny and sad stories about both weddings and funerals. Just as you think you have experienced everything, something new happens that exceeds what you thought was the limit of possibility. This is an example of the fact that the pastor is truly a general practitioner with access to, and concern for, every aspect of persons' lives. You will learn things about people that no one else knows, and see families in their most vulnerable moments. The pastor is required by ordination vows to maintain absolute confidentiality, so that the tensions and problems revealed in individual counseling sessions, or family meetings, are never known by anyone else.

Despite all the rapid change, our culture still seeks the kind of total pastoral care that the occasions of weddings, funerals, and other special events allow. The central act is the service of worship over which the pastor presides. It is the service which brings everything together, that people remember, and to which they return continually in conversation. The pastoral role goes beyond the service to all that comes before and after; but it is the pastor's role as worship leader that opens the door for other ministry.

5. *The pastor as theologian.* A theologian is one who is able to see the activity of God in all aspects of human existence. The pastor is expected to think theologically, and interpret the theological meaning of daily events. There are many "helping professionals" who care deeply for people, and are skilled in providing services of various kinds. Most unique about the pastor is the specific affirmation of the theological meaning and significance of life.

Even though a pastor's rigorous scholarly theological training may not always be displayed, it is nevertheless present, and informs the reflective practice of ministry. One of the enduring contributions of the Reformation understanding of the minister as theologian, especially in the Lutheran and Reformed traditions, is the insistence that the pastor must always seek to know the theological implications of decisions, involvements, and programs of the church and its ministry.

A responsible pastor will ask theological questions about everything; and be able to help other Christians learn to do the same. Pastors are asked to do all sorts of things that seem nice and appropriate to people. One of the roles of the pastor is to engage in clear theological thinking about all such requests. The integrity of Christian ministry requires that the one who is set aside to lead provide theological help to the community for its own good. This is the reason the community designates some of its number for this service.

6. *The pastor as teacher.* Presbyterian churches historically referred to the pastor as the "teaching elder." All pastors are called to the teaching office. Theological education is pursued so that ordained ministers will be capable of serving in this role. A major component of the pastor's work is to be the "lead" teacher in the congregation. In most cases it is neither

necessary nor possible for the pastor to be the only teacher. There are capable lay persons, many of whom are well-equipped to teach. Too often, however, teaching has not been viewed as central to the pastor's role; and the educational ministry of the church has not been given adequate attention. Many Christians are woefully ignorant of the rudiments of the faith.

The pastor is charged to be sure that all members of the congregation have the opportunity to learn more about the Bible, the historical development of the church, church teachings about Christian faith and life, and ways Christians think about contemporary happenings. The ordained minister is expected to be visibly present as a teacher in the congregation, and to be a resource for materials and ideas. Sometimes this will involve teaching the other teachers in the church. Sometimes it will mean direct service in classes. It will always include teaching classes for those seeking baptism, for baptized Christians who are changing congregations or traditions, and for young people who have grown up in the church, preparing to affirm for themselves vows made at their baptism.

Not all teaching occurs in a classroom setting. The teaching office includes teaching that is done by example as the pastor engages in the multiple activities demanded in church and community. The Scriptures admonish us to "be examples to the flock" (1 Pet. 5:3). Teaching is involved in all of the things that the pastor does, and is central to the meaning of ordained ministry.

*7. The pastor as evangelist.* The role of evangelist is worth noting separately, even though it might well be assumed as part of the preaching and teaching roles. In fact it is related to all aspects of Christian ministry. The reason for listing it separately is to remind ourselves that the proclamation of the gospel of Jesus Christ is a specific mandate to all Christians, and that helping the church to understand proclamation as a part of its total ministry is one duty of the pastor. It is conceivable that pastoral ministry can be confined within the Christian community. The pastor can work full time ministering with those who are already members of the church. Many congregations do little outside the church and never add new members. Such a conception of ministry is inauthentic, because it fails to address a major mandate of the gospel. On the other hand, it is possible to let the push for new members become so all-consuming that it defines a pastor or congregation. The danger is that church growth threatens to become an end in itself, especially when it borrows techniques and judgments from secular marketing. The gospel should not be offered as if it were a product.

Evangelization is part of the wholeness of Christian ministry. It must not be ignored. Every pastor needs to attend to the mandate to spread the gospel, and invite others to join the Christian community.

*8. The pastor as pastoral caregiver and counselor.* Part of a pastor's day is spent ministering to people who are in need of pastoral care and counseling. This may take place in homes, hospitals, the pastor's study, work places, or places of incidental meeting. The care and counseling given by the pastor is different from that given by anyone else. The modifier "pastoral" means that the care is given not just by a "helping professional" but by an ordained minister of the church. Pastoral care is not the ministry of an individual but of the whole community of Jesus Christ, because the pastor is its official representative, and authorized to minister in its name.

If you are an ordained minister you will spend most of your time out among people. Every day there will be one or more home visits. A pastoral call is not just a friendly chat. It usually involves a prior appointment, so that the individual or family will be home and prepared to greet you. It is an occasion for the pastor to learn something new about the life circumstances of those visited, and to offer some dimension of the church's ministry to that situation. Often specific needs will be mentioned, or comments made that the pastor will want to remember. Ideas about the life of the congregation or questions about the faith may be discussed. If there are children in the home the pastor will be certain to give them some time. The visit ordinarily lasts no more than half an hour and will end with a time of prayer.

You will sometimes hear people say that the day of pastoral visits to homes is over. People are too busy, it is too difficult to get around, it is an inefficient use of time; the excuses are endless. In fact, people are hungry for pastoral presence in the home. Loneliness and alienation characterize the lives of many people. According to the 1990 census, more than 22 million Americans live alone. That is twelve percent of the nation, compared with seven percent reported in the 1980 figures. The *Journal of the American Medical Association* reports that many of those people are so lonely and depressed that they are dying of isolation. Homes in which single parents are trying to deal with the complexities of family life, and traditional families seeking to deal with the demands of contemporary society, seek conversation and communication with a thoughtful pastor. Pastoral visitation may be more important than ever. When I talk with lay persons I can tell instantly how a pastor is doing. Effective pastors do not work in offices; their reading and preparation is done in the study; otherwise, they are out among the people. Pastoral visitation in homes is one of the chief ways the pastor ministers to whole persons. Parishioners have lives outside of the church building. If the pastor only sees them there, he or she has a limited picture and falls into the trap of the "modern professional" who specializes in only one part of life. Home visitation keeps the pastor in touch with the people on their own turf, and alive to the realities of the community. Questions encountered and conversations shared will subtly influence preaching and teaching, allowing both to better meet the needs of the parish.

Visitation in hospitals continues the pastoral role of caring for the sick. Modern hospitals are so threatening and alienating that patients and their families are often frightened and bewildered. The presence of the pastor is comforting in the ordinary human sense. But the pastor is not there simply as a friend. Significant pastoral counseling for the patient and the patient's family frequently takes place in the hospital. The pastor represents the coming of Christ and the church to the patient's hospital room. The theological meaning of a hospital visit is that the prayers of the church to God, shared in the hospital room by the pastor, the sick person, and perhaps family members, are a powerful and necessary ingredient in the total well-being of the patient. This is the case in times of joy and thanksgiving as well as in times of anxiety and sorrow. The work of the Holy Spirit uplifts the patient and family as the focus is turned away from the immediacy of physical illness, even sickness unto death, to the abiding mercy and sustaining grace of God. The pastor's prayers and presence remind the patient and family of God's providence in both health and sickness, life and death.

Problems relating to marriage, children, parents, work, church relationships, and an almost endless number of topics, also regularly end up in the pastor's study when persons request a time to come and talk. Sometimes a chance encounter on the sidewalk, or in a store, will be the occasion for pastoral care. The pastor is sought for advice, because it is often spiritual counsel that is really wanted when one is in need. All ordained ministers are trained in the basic rudiments of pastoral care and counseling, often including fine programs of clinical pastoral education. Most do not receive advanced clinical training in therapy. Therefore the pastor will know to refer some parishioners to other persons who can meet specific critical needs. The pastor always remembers that the unique offering of the ordained minister is not social service or psychological counsel but the ministry of the church, which points us beyond our selfish interests, even in times of extraordinary trial, to God and God's people.

Part of the pastoral care of the church is being attentive to the work of the Holy Spirit in calling other persons to ordained ministry. An imperative of ordained ministry is to help pass the call on to others. The pastor keeps an eye out for persons of unusual gifts and graces for ministry and talks with them about God's claim on their lives.

*9. The pastor as orderer of congregational life.* Congregations expect their pastor to be an effective administrator of the life of the church; but the ordering role has theological significance that goes well beyond management. Congregations have institutional and organizational needs. They are human communities which operate in some ways as any other organization. But the term *orderer* does not mean that the pastor "gives orders." It means that the pastor helps bring order to the life of the church. Without order there is chaos, whether in nature or in human interaction. God brought order in the act of creation; and so we talk about the "natural order." God gives the possibility of ordering human community so that human sin does not triumph and bring about chaos and destruction. The theological significance of ordering is that good order allows all persons to use their gifts to participate and contribute to the needs of the whole in appropriate ways. The pastor exercises the ordering task on behalf of the congregation so that it can be about its primary work of ministry in the name of Jesus Christ.

Great damage can be done to a congregation by an inept

pastor who does not understand, or is unable to carry out, the ordering role. You will be expected to learn how to manage the multiple aspects of parish life. There is much to be learned from contemporary management theory. One of these is that management is never for its own sake. This is obviously so in the case of the church. You will learn to lead in such a way that administration, in a sense, becomes invisible. Good management does not mean spending large amounts of time behind a desk in a church office. Just the opposite is the case. Sometimes office work is an excuse for avoiding the really important demands of ministry. If you want to maintain regular office hours, you should not seek ordination as a pastor. Much of the day-to-day management of the church can be done by lay persons, whether the congregation is small or large. Your job will be to coordinate that work, and see to it that it is accomplished, not necessarily to do it yourself. The pastor's role is to be present out among the people helping the community work together through good communication and open participation, and to identify, recruit, and train laity for service. The key is constantly keeping before the congregation the priority of the ministry for which the administration is being done.

The pastoral role of ordering the life of the congregation suggests that there are rules, or guidelines, by which this ordering is done. This we call church "polity." *Polity* comes from the same root as *politics*. You will often hear that the church is full of "politics." This is meant to be a derogatory remark about the nature and character of the church. Of course the church is full of "politics," for the church is in part a human community, and any human community is full of "politics." In the best sense of the word, politics is about the shaping of communal life for the good of the whole, according to guidelines established to protect both individuals and the group. Communities are well-served if they have clear guidelines governing their common life.

Church polity refers to the way a specific community of Christians shapes its life to carry out ministry. It is essential to understand that theology and polity cannot be separated. The study of church polity involves learning about the way the particular church tradition in which you seek ordination orders its life. These matters are not incidental. There are powerful theological reasons that determine the way different church bodies order their life. Specific interpretations of Scripture and teaching result in Catholic, Orthodox, or Protestant expressions of the church; and within each of these there are differences that result from diverse theological insights, as well as historical developments, and differing geographical and social settings. Within Protestantism, for instance, there are a wide variety of polities. Methodists, Lutherans, Episcopalians, Baptists, Congregationalists, and Presbyterians each have characteristic polities. Methodism, with its strong emphasis on connectional polity and episcopal appointment of ordained ministry, for instance, is strikingly different from the Southern Baptist tradition of radical congregational independence. Two things need to be emphasized. The first is that polity is not simply a matter of organizational preference. Different polities convey different thinking and claims about the nature of the church, and the way ministry is carried out in the world. In thinking about ordained ministry, one needs to learn about these theological understandings and think deeply about them. The second follows directly from the first. In accepting the church's call to ordained ministry, one takes responsibility for ministering within a specific tradition of Christianity. This means that part of the ordering role is leading the congregation to shape its life in conformity to the larger tradition in which it stands, and to understand and affirm that particular Christian tradition. The pastor needs to remember and communicate the theological insights embodied in polity, so that the ordering role has integrity.

*10. The pastor as public figure.* If you are a pastor, you are a public figure. The phrase "public figure" has meaning both inside and outside the church. Within the church community you will perform the leadership role of presiding on most communal occasions. We covered this in considering the presidential role in sacramental celebrations, the role of worship leadership, and the role of ordering the life of the congregation. As a public figure, you will also lead the congregation in its concern for life in the larger community. Ministry is not just what goes on within the congregation, but involves the work of the congregation in the multiple needs of the society. Most urgently these include the passion of the Christian church for social justice, in such areas as the needs of children, racial justice, housing, education, and the eradication of violence and crime. Attention to these concerns is accomplished through individual service on the part of members of the church, through group projects of the church, through intervention in the social and political life of the community, and through pastoral presence in many arenas.

Ordained ministerial leadership can be a powerful ingredient in improving life in society; and the pastor cannot ignore this aspect of service. The clergy plays a role on many boards and agencies of the community outside the church. They are there because they have expertise in working with people and identifying needs. They are also there because they represent an important spiritual reality, which may not be well-articulated by the larger community but nevertheless is felt. There are some needs of society which can never be met by social policy changes or economic reordering. These have to do with the basic issues of meaning and purpose, giving and service. The pastor's role as public figure will sometimes be quiet involvement, sometimes vocal intervention, but it will always include symbolizing the concern and presence of the church in the many arenas of secular society that are so desperately in need of the vision and hope that it alone can give.

### How Can Anyone Do All of These Things?

There are usually two reactions from persons considering the ordained ministry when they think about the diverse and multiple opportunities, expectations, demands, and challenges which are part of the work. One reaction is exhilaration. It is hard to imagine work that is so endlessly interesting and rewarding. Every day new needs and possibilities present themselves; and there are always things to do within the congregation, in the larger church, and in the community. The other reaction is apprehension. How can anyone do all of these things? The work seems to demand a range of ability and expertise that goes beyond what can be expected of all but a few persons. As you reflect on the work of the pastor, it will help you to remember that you are not alone in your decision, and that you will not be alone in the ministry. This is so for the following three reasons:

**God and the church call to ordained ministry persons who have the capacity to do the work.** Remember what we said about the nature of ordained ministry. It is not an occupation chosen in isolation, or simply because it seems attractive. Ordained ministry is a vocation into which God and the church call persons. Ordained ministry is a privilege; and there will be ample opportunity for you to test your call in relationship to both God and the Christian community. The process of discernment will bring you to conviction about your ability and appropriateness for the work. A bit of apprehension is a good thing; pride is devastating in the ministry; but too much apprehension can be paralyzing. No congregation wants an uncertain or tentative pastor who does not seem to know what to do. The calling of the pastor is to instill confidence in the community as it seeks to live the gospel. You need not be fearful, because you are not alone. Jesus Christ is the foundation of our confidence. Bold leadership is needed by the church as it moves into the future to minister in this broken world. Such leadership will be given by God; and you are invited to be part of it.

**One learns constantly to reflect on priorities, and to keep a clear focus on what is most important.** There are not enough hours in the day to do everything. In theological education, in internships of supervised ministry, and in the practice of ordained ministry, you will learn how to evaluate and handle multiple demands. It is evident that some things must take precedence. There is no way specific guidelines can be given, because no two situations are ever identical. The priority of theological reflection on ministry, however, should be obvious. One of the key affirmations of the gospel is that we have freedom for ministry, so we can establish priorities. The effective and responsible pastor will always be capable of articulating, at least privately, why certain claims must come first. These have to do with those things unique to the role of ordained minister; and one learns how to keep a clear focus so that the daily demands do not become overwhelming.

**We trust that God's grace will give us the competence to perform authentic ministry in the name of Jesus Christ and the church.** Professional ministry is a gift from God. We have made it clear that there are some abilities with which we are born, and some that are cultivated through education and training. At the same time, we must remember that these human dimensions are not enough to understand or explain ministry. Without this affirmation the whole enterprise does not make sense. This is the reason that the role of the clergy can be misunderstood by those who do not see through the eyes of faith. It is also the reason why, despite dreadful mistakes and human sin on the part of some ordained ministers, the office of ordained ministry endures. It is not just a human creation to provide organizational leadership; it is a God-given reality to communicate life-saving grace. This recognition reminds us that, though the work of the pastor is exciting, it can also seem overwhelming; but the competence to do the work is a God-given competence, and therefore the possibilities are endless. The Scriptures put it rightly: "Our competence is from God, who has made us competent to be ministers of a new covenant" (2 Cor. 3:5-6).

CHAPTER

5

# The Heart of the Matter: "How Will I Answer the Question?"

*And how are they to believe in one of whom they have never heard? And how are they to hear without someone to proclaim him? And how are they to proclaim him unless they are sent? As it is written, "How beautiful are the feet of those who bring good news!"*

—Romans 10:14-15

### The Gospel Imperative

You now have a picture of ordained ministry. You have considered the ministry of the whole people of God, and the particular ministry of the ordained. You have looked at what it means to be ordained, and the nature of such ministry. You have some idea of the work of the pastor, and what the various responsibilities and tasks include. Now you come to the heart of the matter. The question is now before you. God and the church ask: "Who will go for us?" How will you answer the question?

Never lose sight of the fact that what motivates all consideration of ordained ministry is the imperative of the Christian gospel. Your effort to discern the nature of your vocation takes place in the context of the church, and the commission it received from Jesus Christ: "And Jesus came and said to them, 'All authority in heaven and on earth has been given to me. Go therefore and make disciples of all nations, baptizing them in the name of the Father and of the Son and of the Holy Spirit and teaching them to obey everything that I have commanded you. And remember, I am with you always, to the end of the age' " (Matt. 28:18-20).

**The gospel imperative is a message from God.** The news the church has to share is *revealed* truth received as a gift to God's people. This distinguishes the message from the multiple claims and prescriptions for human well-being that constantly vie for attention and allegiance. In any bookstore you can find hundreds of "self-help" books authored by people who claim to know the answer to human needs and problems. They are always the best sellers because they purport to answer difficult questions in a simple and straightforward manner. H. L. Mencken once remarked, "To every important problem there are ten simple answers. All of them wrong." Although the gospel message is readily understandable, it is not simple-minded; and it certainly is not easily put into action. It does not propose a "quick fix." Christian proclamation is good news that demands individual and communal change, sacrifice, and obedience unto death. Even the best marketing experts have found that these mandates are very costly and difficult to package. That is why misguided efforts at church marketing will water down the gospel to make it more palatable. That kind of packaging is neither honest nor helpful, because real joy and benefit come in direct proportion to the extent of one's selfless commitment and service.

How is the revealed gospel imperative known? In the face of so many, sometimes crazy, proposals, how do we distinguish God's true message? The answer is in the Bible, as interpreted by the church, and in the living tradition of the church. While one can find a huge number of interpretations of the Bible, there is a primary tradition of interpretation which shapes and characterizes the major branches of Christianity. Within the primary tradition is an openness to change, as the Holy Spirit brings about new understandings in new times and settings. The primary tradition is not static, nor is it individualistic, because it is perpetually tested within faithful and intentional Christian community. The experience of the church in its encounter with the Holy Spirit opens new possibilities consistent with God's enduring message for humankind, as well as with insights derived from the work of women and men in contemporary research.

The ordained minister is called to learn about the historical development and current reality of the primary tradition, which seeks to set forth apostolic teaching in a faithful manner. This does not take away the creativity and individuality of the pastor, but these are always tested and modified by the church. In times when religious expression is so often confused, and the witness of authentic Christianity can be clouded by cultic and splinter groups, it is especially important that ordained ministry be responsible to the gospel as it is shared by the historic core and vital presence of Christian faith and witness. The pastor is the servant of God's living Word entrusted to the faithful community of the church.

**The gospel imperative is personalized in Jesus Christ.** Christianity is rooted in the life, death, and resurrection of Jesus of Nazareth. In Jesus, God became human, and God's message was lived out in the world. Jesus exemplified servant ministry, being obedient unto death. In his death on the cross, Christ took unto himself the sins of the whole world; and in his resurrection, the truth of God's ultimate love was proven and certified. The crucifixion and resurrection together are the centerpiece of history. In them the truth of reality is revealed for all time. The Christian proclamation therefore is inseparable from Christ himself. The ordained minister is an ambassador for Jesus Christ and the bearer of God's message in Christ for the sake of others. "And how are they to believe in one of whom they have never heard? And how are they to hear without someone to proclaim him?" (Rom. 10:14). The motivation of the ordained minister is neither self-glory nor self-gratification. The servanthood of Christ is the only authentic model. "For we do not proclaim ourselves; we proclaim Jesus Christ as Lord and ourselves as your slaves for Jesus' sake" (2 Cor. 4:5).

**The gospel imperative is sustained by the Holy Spirit.** Through the work of the Holy Spirit, God moves constantly in the world to bring forth faith, obedience, love, and service. The Holy Spirit brought the church into being, and preserves it through all time. The inspiration of the Spirit is the source of the Scriptures, and of subsequent Christian teaching in the form of the church's creedal statements, the primary teaching tradition, and new insights allowing for change and development. For two thousand years, millions of Christians have been guided into the faith, and preserved in lives of commitment and ministry, by the Holy Spirit. All Christian ministry depends on God's Spirit for authenticity and effectiveness. In the act of ordination, the church asks for the grace and presence of the Spirit to confirm the vocation of those who are set aside for the particular ministry of Word, sacrament, and order.

**The gospel imperative is lived and communicated by the church.** The presence of the church embodies Christian faith, life, and practice for the sake of the whole world. The gospel does not exist in abstract ideas; it is manifested in the actual reality of the church's life and ministry. Though as a human community the church is sinful and limited, as the body of Christ in the world, the church is spiritually power-ful and transcendent in a way invisible to all but those who have the eyes of faith. The community of God's people is called to live in such a way that the gospel is shown forth in daily life through ministries of love and reconciliation. To aid in this mission, the church is given the leadership of ordained ministry, by and through the grace of God. The importance and significance of ordained ministry therefore cannot be overstated. It is necessary for the continuing vitality of the community that embodies the gospel, God's saving message, personalized in Jesus Christ, and sustained by the Holy Spirit.

**The gospel imperative is for all the world.** Following the example of Jesus, the life and work of the church is not for its own sake, but for the sake of the world. This means that the servant ministry of the church is done for others, and that others are invited to share the vision, and join the commu-nity. There are no bounds to the church's ministry; and there are no bounds to the proclamation of the gospel. Proclama-tion requires persons who respond to the call to commit themselves to work toward God's intended order. The shape of that order, as revealed in the Scriptures, is real and present now; but it will be fully realized only in God's own time. The gospel has ultimate significance, therefore, for both individu-als and the whole creation. The urgency of ordained ministry is recognized only when the heart of the matter, the gospel imperative, is kept clearly in view. Ordained ministry is truly work that matters.

### Work That Matters

One night I received a telephone call from a man I had known for a number of years. He told me that his son, Charles, who was 34, felt called to ordained ministry. After consultation with his own pastor, he was trying to decide where to apply for theological education. The father was concerned about the decision, and was calling to see if I would be willing to talk to his son. After agreeing to do so, I found out that the son was married and had two young sons. I called him directly and suggested that he and his wife come to see me. Although it involved a four-hour drive, they came to my office the following Friday afternoon. They were both attractive and articulate. It was evident that these were people of experience and sophistication. After we had some initial conversation, I asked him to tell me his story.

Just before they married, he had gone to work for a well-known manufacturer of home products for kitchens, bathrooms, and personal hygiene. He had risen rapidly to be marketing director for a major division of the company. Especially in the early years of his career, they had moved often. In each community they were active in the church. Increasingly, he told me, he was finding his work in the congregation more satisfying than his work in marketing. What really bothered him was the pressure he had to put on his sales force to push the product. He could do it. His division led the corporation; but he wondered whether he wanted to do it. He commented, "I began to ask myself whether what I was saying was really true. Was our product really that essential? I know, of course, that it wasn't. What real difference did it make whether we sold the product? The only things that mattered were the sales numbers for each quarter, showing we were meeting and exceeding our quota, and the total dollars earned by the division. I began to think that what really mattered were the motivations that drove my ambition."

This story is typical of many mid-career women and men who respond to the call to ordained ministry. I offered a strong case for the marketing job. Many people are employed; the product is useful; it is one piece of the larger economic picture for the whole society. I emphasized that a change at his age, especially with a family, would not be easy. He granted that a Christian could honorably do his present work, and that such a drastic change was not without uncertainties. Nevertheless, he insisted that his mind was made up. If the church would have him, he would offer himself for ordination. His wife was fully supportive. Toward the end of the visit he said, "I want to give my life for work that matters."

One of the true joys of ordained ministry is the daily conviction that the ministry of Jesus Christ has ultimate significance. I reminded him that there would be many aspects of the pastorate that are far from ultimate. As with any human activity, there are things about the work of ministry that seem almost trivial. He was right to recognize, however, that the meaning and purpose of the ministry of the church matters deeply to individuals, communities, and the whole society. By the second year of his seminary experience, he came to the settled conviction that he made the right choice. Despite family dislocation, his wife and sons, who had shared in the decision, were thriving as a result of the new life they experienced together. Several years after he began serving full time as a pastor, he told me that his only regret was that he had not started sooner. If one is convinced of the soundness of the call to ordained ministry, the sooner one begins the journey, the better.

### The Question Always Comes Back

"Who will go for us?" is a question for all Christians. This phrasing allows us to see that there is a dimension of the call from God, and a dimension from God's people. It is also compelling. Once one is convinced of the gospel imperative, sees the needs, and recognizes the challenges and opportunities of the ordained ministry, the question will not go away. It always comes back.

I have a friend named George Snyder, who is a devout Christian and successful businessman. He is fascinated by the kind of persons who enter the ministry. We have long conversations about the nature of ordained ministry, and the financial needs of ministerial students for scholarship support, so that they do not go too deeply into debt. He has been generous in contributing to endowments for student aid because he knows that pastors will not usually have large financial resources. Particularly puzzling to him is why candidates for ordination give up the possibilities of more lucrative careers. One observation he made was especially striking. He told me that he had known many ministers well, and that most of them could have been "wildly successful" in business careers. They had all the gifts, he said, good communication skills, aggressiveness, ambition, insight into people, organizational ability. "Why are they willing to do so much for so little of this world's goods?"

Father Thomas Judge, a Roman Catholic priest of the Vincentian order, was the founder of a small missionary community and seminary originally located in Holy Trinity, Alabama, in the early decades of the twentieth century. The demands on those who responded to the call were great; but the quality of service was high. Paul Hendrickson, in a book called *Seminary,* quotes Father Judge: "Men who for the mere nod could possess kingdoms discarded the tawdry raiment of the world to clothe themselves in the livery of Jesus Christ" (New York: Summit Books, 1983, pp. 236-37). The claim is perhaps a bit overstated, but Father Judge points to a reality many have observed. Whether kingdoms of this world could have been possessed with a mere nod, or whether it might have taken strenuous work, it is a fact that God has always called to the ministry persons of extraordinary ability who might indeed have been tremendously successful in secular occupations. George Snyder's question remains: "Why?"

The answer is powerful. It has remade many lives. As Charles said to me, with candor and simplicity, that day in my office: "I am called to witness to the truth that life does not begin and end in the things of this world, but in the transcendent reality of God." This is why persons offer themselves. Those who serve in ordained ministry sense an irresistible uniting of their talents and abilities with the needs and hopes of the church, through the activity of God's Holy Spirit. The conviction of God's call will not go away. Like an eternal flame, it cannot be extinguished. The joy of Christian community reinforces the sense of urgency. Occasionally persons seek to run away, by denying or rejecting the reality of the call, but there is a strong tugging at the inner being which relentlessly keeps the question alive.

The southeastern corner of Ohio includes a number of counties hit very hard by economic problems. Small towns evidence the poverty and social problems characteristic of the region. The stores on the once-prosperous main streets are run-down and display cheap merchandise. Many buildings are boarded up. In at least one town there is a dramatic exception. Toward the middle of the main street is the best-kept building in town: a church built in 1910. You can tell just by looking that it is the center of town activities. In addition to its predictable ministries, the church offers day care for children, a community-based social program for the elderly, and programs for teenagers, who have little to do, and slim hopes for the future unless they leave the county. The congregation was instrumental in starting an off-site shelter for battered women, to meet a serious need in the troubled county.

The pastor, whose name is Dorothy, has become central

not only to her own congregation, but to the whole town. Her vision, energy, and drive are infectious. During her undergraduate years, she was challenged by the campus pastor to think about ordained ministry. It was the farthest thing from her mind. She was too ambitious, too determined to improve society. Participation in a spiritual life group during her senior year challenged her to think about where she could really use her energies; but she resisted professional ministry. Nevertheless the challenge and reality of call would not go away. The question always came back. Only gradually did she admit to the conviction that God was calling her to give herself for others through service as a pastor. Her parents were doubtful, her friends astonished; but she entered seminary committed to offer herself for ministry in just such a rural, poor county as she now serves. Her presence there has been transformative for the congregation and the whole community. She is convinced that God wants her where she is; and that only through work in specific communities, on modest projects, will society be improved.

The foundation of everything that Dorothy is involved in is her faith in Jesus Christ, and her belief that the ministry of the church offers the greatest hope for humankind, because it alone addresses whole persons and all aspects of life. "It seemed so implausible to think that I might be called to ministry. I resisted, preferring a more conventional life. At last I made the decision to seek ordination, but I was embarrassed to tell anyone. Now I know that I am truly called. The key is my own spiritual growth and service as pastor. I am excited and fulfilled by the total life of ministry, even at those times when I am tired and lonely." The life of service has brought unimagined rewards.

A contemporary hymn by Fred Pratt Green, titled "Whom Shall I Send?" is based on Isaiah 6:8:

*How Will I Answer the Question?*

Whom shall I send? Our Maker cries;
and many, when they hear God's voice,
are sure where their vocation lies;
but many shrink from such a choice.

The phrase "many shrink from such a choice" is haunting. There are all kinds of reasons that can be given: uncertainty about what is expected, fear about worthiness, lack of confidence in one's abilities, doubt that ordained ministry is sufficiently compelling. At base, however, one shrinks from such a choice because there will be demands and expectations that go beyond personal desires and self-gratification. To shrink from the choice for this reason is unsatisfying. God gives the strength and resolve to meet the challenges; and, ironically, positive response to the call to ordained ministry brings not only resolution but also personal fulfillment. It is not that once a decision is made there will be no doubts or difficulties. Trials of multiple sorts are an inevitable part of any significant venture. But there will be immense satisfaction that one is doing work that matters; and such satisfaction is worth more than any transient goods or positions, because it is enduring. One of the paradoxical truths of Christianity is that faithful commitment and service bring joy and peace. Ministry is satisfying work that also returns exceptional rewards to those who serve.

If you are encountered by the call of God and the call of the church to ordained ministry, you need not shrink from such a choice. You do not go forward alone. Again, in the words of Fred Pratt Green:

And yet, believing God who calls
knows what we are and still may be,
our past defeats, our future falls,
we dare to answer: Lord send me!

Those who are called God purifies,
and daily gives us strength to bend

123

our thoughts, our skills, our energies,
and life itself to this one end.

God's grace along the way sustains authentic ministry. Through the initial response to the call, through days of preparation, and in the practice of ministry, you are not alone. As in the case of ancient Israel, the Lord will go in front of you, in a pillar of cloud by day, and in a pillar of fire by night, to give you light, to travel by day and by night. Some are privileged to be called by God and the church to ordained ministry. So the question always comes back: "Who will go for us?" If you perceive the call, do not hesitate in your response: "Here I am, Lord, send me."

# Suggestions for Further Reading

Baxter, Richard. *The Reformed Pastor.* New York: T. Mason and G. Lane, 1837.

Bernier, Paul. *Ministry in the Church: A Historical and Pastoral Approach.* Mystic, Connecticut: Twenty-Third Publications, 1992.

Brown, William Adams. *The Minister, His World and His Work.* Nashville: Cokesbury Press, 1937.

Burrows, William R. *New Ministries: The Global Context.* Maryknoll, New York: Orbis, 1981.

Campbell, Dennis M. *The Yoke of Obedience: The Meaning of Ordination in Methodism.* Nashville: Abingdon Press, 1988.

Carroll, Jackson W. *As One with Authority: Reflective Leadership in Ministry.* Louisville: Westminster/John Knox Press, 1991.

Cooke, Bernard. *Ministry to Word and Sacraments: History and Theology.* Philadelphia: Fortress Press, 1976.

Harrisville, Roy A. *Ministry in Crisis: Changing Perspectives on Ordination and the Priesthood of All Believers.* Minneapolis: Augsburg, 1987.

Herbert, George. *A Priest to the Temple, or Parson.* London: Methuen, 1899.

Holmes, Urban T. *The Priest in Community: Exploring the Roots of Ministry.* New York: Seabury, 1978.

Manson, T. W. *The Church's Ministry.* Philadelphia: Westminster Press, 1948.

McBrien, Richard P. *Ministry: A Theological, Pastoral Handbook.* San Francisco: Harper and Row, 1987.

Niebuhr, H. Richard. *The Purpose of the Church and Its Ministry.* New York: Harper and Row, 1956.

Nouwen, Henri W. *The Living Reminder: Service and Prayer in Memory of Jesus Christ.* New York: Seabury Press, 1977.

Oden, Thomas C. *Pastoral Theology: Essentials of Ministry.* San Francisco: Harper and Row, 1983.

Oman, John. *Concerning the Ministry.* London: SCM Press, 1936.

Power, David M. *Ministers of Christ and His Church: The Theology of the Priesthood.* London: Geoffrey Chapman, 1969.

Pragman, James H. *Traditions of Ministry: A History of the Doctrine of the Ministry in Lutheran Theology.* St. Louis: Concordia, 1983.

Ramsey, Michael. *The Christian Priest Today.* London: SPCK, 1987.

Schillebeeckx, Edward. *The Church with a Human Face: A New and Expanded Theology of Ministry.* New York: Crossroad, 1985.